SWITZERLAND:

HISTORICAL AND DESCRIPTIVE.

"What lonely magnificence stretches around!
Each sight how sublime! and how awful each sound!
All hush'd and serene, as a region of dreams,
The mountains repose 'mid the roar of the streams;
Their glens of black umbrage by cataracts riven,
But calm their blue tops in the beauty of heaven."

New-York:
PUBLISHED BY CARLTON & PORTER,
SUNDAY-SCHOOL UNION, 200 MULBERRY-STREET.
1856.

CONTENTS.

PART I.—HISTORICAL.

PART II.—DESCRIPTIVE.

SWITZERLAND:

HISTORICAL AND DESCRIPTIVE.

PART I.—HISTORICAL.

CHAPTER I.

THE DIM DISTANCE.

The aboriginal inhabitants of the beautiful land, to some account of which this volume is devoted, were doubtless the bear, the wolf, and the chamois. Wild animals originally roamed at will among its rocks and ravines, through its woods and forests, along its valleys and table-lands, over its glaciers and snow mountains. Perfectly uncultivated, barren in many parts, but yielding here and there profuse vegetation in forms most diversified, the whole aspect of the country must have been as wild as its wandering tenants. Nowhere has human toil and skill been more active and ingenious than in Switzerland, in tilling the soil and reclaiming the waste, and in gathering round the savage scenes of nature the pleasing forms of civilization. What a country of awful and terrible grandeur must it have been before man had begun to fell its trees, to lay out fields and towns on the banks of its rivers, and to make paths over its mountains! What an impression must its vast solitudes have made on the minds of those who were first led by the accidents of war or the chase to penetrate into its unknown recesses!

The earliest human inhabitants were probably of the Celtic race. "Cimmerian darkness" has become proverbial. The Cimmerian and the Celt appear to be the same, and the clouds and gloom with which ancient popular belief overspread the regions peopled by them, ere they spread over the heart of Europe, are but emblematical of the deep obscurity which envelops all their early movements. While classical and other nations on the Mediterranean shores, and kingdoms and empires in the East, were in a state of advanced civilization, with historians recording their national progress, these Celtic emigrants, who found a home among the fastnesses of the Alps, were rude and barbarous; unorganized, and not attaining to the rank of a national existence; ignorant of the higher laws of social life, and incapable of recording their own struggles.

The first glimpse we catch of this Celtic people

is at a period about a century before the Christian era, under the name of Helvetians. Cæsar subsequently alludes to them as strong and warlike, and specially distinguishes two tribes of them, the Tigurini and the Urbigeni, whose local position it has been supposed were Zurich and Orbe. In addition to the Celtic Helvetii, who settled or wandered about the northern and western regions of the Alps, there was a distinct race, perhaps of Etruscan origin, who inhabited the present Grison country, called Rhætia by the Romans. The Tigurinian Helvetii, if we may so call them, we find, in the time of the Consul L. Cassius, engaged in an invasion of Gaul, fighting in union with the Cimbri, also of the Cimmerian or Celtic stock. Cassius was sent against them, for Gaul had become subject to Roman sway. A battle was fought between these people and the consular army; on the banks of the Aar, say some; on the eastern shore of Lake Leman, say others; but it is agreed by all that the consul was killed and the Romans routed. A Celtic leader named Divico appears conspicuously in connection with this exploit of the hardy mountaineers, and after him another chieftain, still more remarkable, called Orgetorix. He seems to have been a man of ambition, discontented with a mountain life, preferring the pursuits of war to the feeding of his cattle, and turning his eyes with envy from the wastes around to the well-tilled fields of Gaul. Oratory is numbered among his gifts; and as the result of his persuasive eloquence, his people are described as resolving to emigrate with all their possessions in search of a richer home. Selfish and despotic designs, however, on the part of this individual, being discovered by his followers, he committed suicide to escape the threatened punishment of the stake. Notwithstanding, the project of settling in Gaul was pursued; but Cæsar met these wanderers and thinned their numbers; sending back those who survived to repair their forsaken and ruined dwellings, and to remember that they were thenceforth tributaries to Rome.

After Gaul was thoroughly subdued, the conquerors sent, in pursuance of their established policy, certain colonies into the country of Helvetia, and for a while some sort of amity existed between the Celtic men of the mountain and their new masters; but a war soon broke out between them. The Roman legions, under Cæcina, aided by the subject Rhætians, attacked with experienced skill and steady valor the undisciplined bands of the Helvetii, cutting them down with resistless force, giving them no quarter, showing them no mercy. Slavery was the lot of those who escaped death; and the poor natives of the rocks and woods had to rue their temerity in daring to face the conquerors of the world. Even surrender did not placate their aroused wrath; and the earliest episode in Helvetian history, which appeals strongly to our feelings, is that of Julia Alpinula, who pleaded in vain with the legate and General Cæcina for the life of her father, when with the people of Aventicum he humbly submitted to the victorious enemy. A touching record of the failure of her personal entreaties in the Roman camp, at the feet of the Roman warrior, was long ago discovered in the following inscription on a stone among the ruins of Aventicum:—"I, Julia Alpinula, lie buried here; the unhappy child of an unhappy father; a priestess of the goddess Aventia. I was unable by my prayers to avert his death, for fate had decreed his mournful end. I have lived three-and-twenty years." The eloquence of Claudius Cossus, a Helvetian envoy, was more successful; and through his representations, acknowledgments, and entreaties, the wrath of the Roman soldiery was appeased, when it was on the point of wreaking summary vengeance on the vanquished, and totally exterminating the race. Better times came afterward, and Vespasian, who had spent his boyhood in the city of the young priestess Julia, enlarged its walls and improved its buildings. Marks of old Roman civilization have been traced over the Rhætian Alps and the open country in the north of Switzerland. The language of the former region at the present day is a proof of the existence there of Roman influence; while Roman stations have been identified in a line from Wallenstadt to Berne, by way of Lucerne. To the south of this boundary it is supposed that Roman power was not steadily employed; and that the Helvetii, who were living there, retained a wild independence.

No incidents are discernible in the dim distance relative to Helvetia for some centuries after the age of Vespasian; but at the fall of the empire, when all Europe appears in movement and confusion, the organization of the old world being broken up, and the elements of the modern world beginning to appear, we discover that fresh tribes were coming from the north to find a home among the Swiss hills and valleys, and to become the parents of the race who since have covered their country with proofs of vigorous industry, and have linked it in enduring association with the romantic stories of their patriotism and valor.

First came the Burgundians from the Baltic shores, settling down between the Jura range, the Lake of Geneva, and the river Aar. Then came the

Alemanni with vengeful hate against all that was Roman, and spread themselves over the northern portions, or what is now called German Switzerland. Then came the Ostrogoths, establishing their power in the Rhætian Alps. Finally came the Franks, crushing the Alemanni, and sharing Switzerland with the Burgundians and Ostrogoths. But the Burgundians had soon to submit to the Franks, and the Ostrogoths were too weak to retain their possessions; so that we find, at the end of the sixth century, all Helvetia had become subject to Frankish sway. It should be observed, however, that the Burgundians remained a distinct people.

The buddings of Roman civilization among the Helvetii were nipped, and the seeds entirely destroyed by this influx of barbarian tribes. Roman architecture and art, with its comforts and luxuries, completely disappeared, especially before the Alemanni, to be replaced, however, in progress of time, by the fruits of a better civilization—attended by social habits of higher and purer morality which would more than compensate for the temporary loss. For a time there was the reign of desolation. The flocks and herds of the new possessors of the land "supplied them with all they required for subsistence, so that the whole country became one vast common or pasture ground; the arable and cultivated lands were abandoned to waste, the furrows of the Roman plow overgrown with thickets, while the banks of the Lake of Constance became covered with vast forests, the retreat of wolves and bears." Thus in many parts men resigned their dominion over nature, and the aboriginal brute denizens of the woods returned to their former haunts.

The Franks, however, brought with them the rudiments of that remarkable social system which formed a rough kind of network during the middle ages—keeping men and things together in some imperfect connection and order. Feudal arrangements obtained in Switzerland from the time of the earliest Frankish settlements; the Frankish king was a feudal sovereign; the Frankish court was a type of the feudal baron; the Frankish soldiers were the precursors and patterns of the feudal vassal; and too many of the old Helvetii who remained were reduced to a state of servitude, and became the progenitors of feudal serfs.* Feudalism did not reach its full organic development till the tenth century, when it was found in France, exhibiting all its characteristic features, and yielding advantages of no mean value in otherwise almost lawless times; but the

* For an account of the feudal system, see "Glimpses of the Dark Ages," No. 365 Youth's Library.

germs of that order of things were certainly springing up among the Franks on their first establishment in Gaul and Helvetia, to produce their ripened fruits after the days of Charlemagne.

The Celts were pagans, and the slaves of abject superstition. They worshiped not only the sun, the moon, and the stars, but the sylphs and shadowy powers which they imagined haunted the wood, the rock, and the stream. The Romans carried their religion along with their arms into Helvetia; but besides the forms of Roman worship, there would still be retained by the natives the adoration of their earlier gods. The date of the introduction of Christianity into Switzerland cannot be ascertained; we have only legends remaining in reference to this important branch of history, and they are anything but safe guides to a definite conclusion. There may be a measure of truth in them; but how, in this case, to separate the gold from the alloy is a process which modern ingenuity is incompetent to discover. We read of Beatus in the first, and of Lucius in the third century, as teachers of the Christian religion to the pagans of Helvetia. No doubt the tidings of the gospel may be regarded as having been conveyed at a very early age, if not by express missionaries, yet by converted soldiers and travelers from Rome, after a Church had been established in that city, to most of the provinces of the empire, especially to one so little remote as Helvetia; and it is pretty certain that Churches existed in the country of the Valais before the end of the fourth century, and in Geneva, Coire, and Aventicum during the fifth. The Franks under Clovis, as the result of their victory over the Alemanni, and in fulfillment of a previous conditional vow, embraced the religion of Christ, to whose interference they attributed their success; but a profession of Christianity under such circumstances is anything but satisfactory, for however sincere the parties might be, they could not have a correct and adequate idea of the faith they nominally embraced. Whatever might be the Christianity of the Franks, no doubt they carried it with them, such as it was, to their new abodes, and diffused it among those who became their subjects and dependents. The Christian religion, under a purer form and by a better agency, was taught to the inhabitants of the north-eastern part of Switzerland at the beginning of the seventh century. It was conveyed by a missionary born in Ireland, and educated under Columba, the founder of the Scottish monastery, in the island of Iona. Less corrupted, and maintained with more zeal and vigor than in some other parts of Europe, Christianity flourished in that remote spot, throwing its illumination far and wide. Trained so auspiciously in an age when primitive Christianity had declined, Gall became the companion of Columba in his missionary enterprises. After attending him in France, he proceeded alone to a place called Arbon, near the Lake of Constance. He finally removed to a retired spot near the river Sitter, where, in company with twelve brethren, he laid the foundation of an institute which afterward became the famous monastery of St. Gall. Some buildings yet remain, the relics of this once powerful establishment; and the name of their original founder still connected with them, after the lapse of so many ages, points to their Gaelic origin—for "the Gael" is evidently the import of the missionary's title—and it thus connects the diffusion of the gospel in that part of Switzerland with Scotland.

It is a curious fact, that the earliest account we have of bell-towers is in the records of the Columban monastery of Iona, from which point they seem to have been spread over other parts of Europe; so that in the line of old towers of that description, between the Rhætian Alps and Cologne, along the banks of the Rhine, may be traced the interesting memorials of missionary labors performed by these Scottish Christians. Ascetic practices, we certainly know, and deeply lament, blended with their piety, for they are characteristic of their age; but if their faith was mixed with error, their devotion seems to have been fervent, and their zeal and activity untiring. The monastery of St. Gall became not only a school of religious instruction, but a center of civilization, in times when, according to the statements just made, humanizing influences were so much needed. As early as the ninth century, a pile of buildings, with which the primitive cells of the Gaelic missionaries could not be compared, succeeded those simple structures. They were of very spacious dimensions, and embraced all the details of a complete and commanding monastic institute. While we can never forget and must deeply deplore that monachism was thoroughly unscriptural in its fundamental principle, and that in many of its religious effects it was extremely pernicious, yet we should remember that the industry of the monks was, in the hands of God's providence, the means of effecting beneficial results to the age in which they lived. We happen to have before us a curious plan of the monastery of St. Gall, as it existed in the ninth century. It illustrates the provisions made in it for the support of the large community dwelling within its walls, and for the aid and benefit of the surrounding inhabitants and the travelers who reached its gates. Judging from the plan, it must have been a little town, full of streets and houses, grouped about a large church. There were shops for numerous trades, including shoemakers, saddlers, turners, curriers, goldsmiths, and fullers. The building included barns and thrashing-floors, with sheds and houses for cattle, sheep, and swine, and ample accommodation for fowls and ducks, to which were added large gardens and goodly orchards, well stocked with vegetables and fruits. Infirmaries and schools were also embraced within its spacious walls; and the hospitium for the entertainment of wayfarers was one of its most characteristic provisions. The monastery of St. Gall, brought so vividly before us by the plan just mentioned, is the one distinct spot in the dim distance of early Swiss civilization.

Charlemagne must be noticed, in connection with this part of our history. The Helvetian territory, as part of the Frankish kingdom, came under his sway. He was a civilizer in a barbarous age; a man seeking, amid manifold confusion, to subdue society into something like order. He had a vigorous mind, a strong arm, and a steady will; and in Switzerland, as well as elsewhere, he sought to improve the condition of his subjects. He promoted agriculture in the valleys, and taught the peasants to clothe the hills with vines. His stay at Zurich is particularly recorded. There he enriched the cathedral and established schools—a branch of national improvement on which, with much wisdom, he especially set his heart; and a work of benevolence which the Zurichers, with sympathetic wisdom, were wont to celebrate by an annual festival.

CHAPTER II.

SEEDS OF NATIONALITY.

Great empires, established by great men, have crumbled away with the dust of their founders. The empire of Charlemagne fell to pieces after his death. Germanic Helvetia, the abode of the old Alemanni, formed part of the great Germanic division which became subject to the scepter of Lothaire. Burgundian Helvetia remained attached to France, under Henry the Fowler, who succeeded to the crown of the German empire at the close of the ninth century. We trace among the inhabitants of Germanic Helvetia, the formation of elements which prepared for the existence and unfolding of Swiss nationality. The emperor was a friend to the foundation and improvement of towns; seeking thereby to establish posts of defense against a new horde of barbarians, the Magyars or natives of Hungary, who were then traversing the old pathway of the Huns, in order to possess themselves of the coveted territory of the west and south. Accordingly, he walled and fortified Soleure, Basle, Zurich, and St. Gall; a town having grown up at the latter spot in the neighborhood of the famous monastery of that name. Corporate councils for deliberation and action were among the fruits of this revived municipal life, of which Henry planted the seeds along the frontiers of the Swiss dominions. The same thing was afterward repeated in that portion of Helvetia which had formerly known the Burgundian rule, and Geneva, Lausanne, and Fribourg were added to the number of the new corporate towns. These civic communities afforded points of attraction to the free inhabitants of the country, whose liberty, owing to the power and oppression of neighboring petty counts and bishops, was most imperfect and uncertain, most disturbed and insecure. The solitary freeman was little better than the serf; but combination in the town, and organized union within its well-built walls, enabled the inhabitants to defend their lives, families, and possessions against the assaults of lordly marauders. They ceased to be either mere units or herds of slaves. They sacrificed a lawless independence; but they found liberty within lines of order, and safety under the shield of mutual protection. Social sympathies took root in their new abodes, as they had not done among the rude and scattered farms of the hill and glen. Individual patriotism, born in the country, shaped itself, within the towns, into social forms; the love of home fired at once a thousand hearts; and affections were cultivated, out of which afterward arose some of the most striking phenomena of Swiss nationality. The population of Helvetia was still comparatively small; the villages were poor and thinly peopled, and the towns were few, and as yet, for the most part, far from strong. But bonds of union are seen in that remote age, at least occasionally and for a time, woven here and there by some one hand more vigorous than others, or by the united action of the less powerful. The house of Zærin-gen appears conspicuous in the history of Switzer-land during the twelfth century. The dukes of that family, who bore the name of Bertholdt, possessed considerable prerogatives delegated to them by the emperor of Germany; and at the same time owed additional power to their being elected as kast vogts, or patrons, by Zurich and other towns. They exercised an indefinable kind of lordship over a large part of Helvetia, but chiefly employed their power in the establishment and protection of towns. They exacted oaths of fidelity from those to whom they gave encouragement, afforded support, or promised defense. The bondsmen, who fled to the towns, are described as "free, when their masters did not claim them within the term of one year, and prove their vassalage by the oath of seven witnesses. The burghers imposed taxes on themselves. In the wars of the duke they were not obliged to march to such a distance as would prevent them from sleeping at home the same night. Every burgher was also obliged to possess a house, as a pledge of his allegiance. In good or evil fortune they stood each for all and all for each."

It is true that the town thus became to the citizen as his country, and patriotism took but a narrow range; yet a schooling was thus going on for the subsequent outgrowths of Helvetic nationality, and the Bertholdts were the nurses of that spirit of mutual league and brotherhood which at length was manifested by the Swiss in their republican confederation. Bertholdt the fifth was the most distinguished of his family, and to him is attributed the erection of Berne, on the lofty peninsula which is formed by the circling stream of the Aar. The position he selected does credit to his taste, and proves his wisdom, while no one who now visits the picturesque old city can fail to notice the honor paid to his memory by the Bernese. One of the favorite legendary stories of the place relates to the origin of its name. Bertholdt is said to have resolved on taking a title for his city from the first animal whom his huntsmen should kill in the chase. A bear was attacked and slaughtered, and hence the appellation of Berne, which signifies *bear*, was given to the spot.

It is difficult sometimes to spell men's motives out of their actions, and perhaps we should be attributing too much to the Bertholdts if we were to describe them as disinterested friends to the liberties of the people; probably they intended by the establishment of towns to strengthen themselves against the rival nobles of their time. But at any rate they proved themselves benefactors to their race, and their names appear with some considerable degree of honor in the early annals of Switzerland.

Upon the extinction of the Zæringen dynasty, another and still more illustrious friend of his country appeared in the person of Rudolph of

Hapsburgh, a member of a family of feudal lords, who had long maintained a wide and powerful rule in the north of Switzerland. Such was his importance and influence, that in 1273 he was elevated to the throne of the German empire; but so far from forgetting the interests of the land of his birth, after his attainment of that distinguished honor, he devoted himself—at least for a while—most sedulously to the improvement of the Helvetic towns, by adding to their municipal privileges; thus walking in the footsteps of the Dukes of Zæringen. To Zurich, Shaffhausen, and Soleure, were conceded by him the right of electing their own judges and framing their own laws. Laupen and Lucerne were placed on a level with Berne; and Bienne was invested with the same immunities as Basle. The latter part of Rudolph's career proved not so favorable to the interests of his countrymen.

While nationality was fostered in the towns, the same sentiment was rising, under very different circumstances, in the rural districts of Helvetia. On the borders of the lake now known as that of the four cantons, dwelt a race of shepherds from ancient times, in a state of primitive simplicity, undisturbed in what was then an almost inaccessible region, strangers to Alemanni, Burgundian, and Frank, and nursing in their breasts a spirit of courage and freedom amid the mountain air and by the mountain stream. Three valleys were in close neighborhood, called Schwyz, Unterwalden, and Uri, forming the Waldstatten, or wooded cantons. According to their own traditions they were from Scandinavia, or Friesland, an island on the North Sea.* They were peopled by inhabitants of a remote northern origin, descendants from one stock, with feelings and traditions in common, strengthened, even after the increase of their flocks had rendered it needful for them to seek fresh pastures, by their continuing still to frequent in the vale of the Muotta the same church within the humble walls of which their fathers had worshiped. When each band of settlers was compelled to have its own house of prayer, its own court of justice, and its own distinct rulers and guardians, a bond of union, derived from their common descent and early associations, was still preserved. Their abodes were so unfrequented by strangers that their existence long remained unknown to the lords of Helvetia; and some of their judicial usages were so simple that they had what was called a street court, which consisted of the first seven men who happened to assemble. In religion, some among them at least seem to be

* Not the modern Friesland.

free from certain errors of their times. In a later chronicle of the Abbey of Corvey, written in the twelfth century, Swiss travelers are mentioned—the people of these forests or wood cantons alone bore the name then—as opposed to image or relic worship, and other rites of the Romish Church, and as knowing the Bible by heart.*

In this very hasty and imperfect sketch of Swiss history, we can dwell only on a few leading points; but to prevent being misunderstood, we must remark, in connection with these notices of the seeds of nationality, that while a process was going on, destined by Divine Providence at length to yield some very remarkable results, there was a great deal coëxistent with that process calculated to hinder its advance. At the time of which we speak, there were to be found over Switzerland at large, numbers of petty tyrants, both lay and ecclesiastical, who were crushing the energies of the feudal dependents by the weight of their exactions, and who looked with intense jealousy upon the proceedings of the Dukes of Zæringen and the Count of Hapsburgh. The reader would make a grievous mistake if he were to suppose either that those distinguished

* Planta gives the passage, from which it appears that some of these people would not eat animal food. —Helvetic Confederacy, vol. i, p. 178.

personages had an uncontested lordship over the land, or that other nobles adopted plans like theirs. A number of counts strove to maintain, and not without success, the utmost amount of feudal authority, and to exact from their vassals all the submissive homage and tribute that could possibly be obtained. The Abbots of St. Gall and of Einsiedlen are mentioned as honorable exceptions, having promoted the welfare of the serfs on their estates by releasing their bonds and by encouraging their industry. Yet in cases when, from enlightened views or with selfish ends, a baron or bishop improved his property and the comfort of his humbler tenants, by commanding them to clear the land, cultivate the soil, and build better homesteads, these poor men, according to feudal usage, so executing their lord's pleasure, did it but as menials, having only a modified and imperfect kind of property in the fruit of their labor. They received "the timber requisite for their dwellings and stables, the seeds for sowing, the plow and wagon for the labors of the field, a hatchet and ladder for those within doors, the first cows in the stall, the first sow and pigs, and in the farm-yard the first cocks and hens. For this they were required to pay a tax on every article, to afford their services in the field for their lord, and transport the products to his castle, to pay rent and tithes for their own crops, and other contributions in linen, cheese, poultry, and eggs."—*Zschokke.*

Among those who were sunk in the lowest state of vassalage were the inhabitants of the Rhætian Alps. The Bishop of Coire, and certain abbots and counts, ruled with a rod of iron over their rural tributaries. Many a castle raised its head in the rocky passes of that rugged but magnificent region, at the foot of which groups of peasants dwelt in a state of miserable serfdom. The old town of Coire enjoyed municipal rights, and in some of the remoter valleys there were people who lived in comparative independence; but generally, in about the whole of what is now the common line of road from Wallenstadt to Splügen Pass, the condition of the inhabitants in the tenth century, and for four hundred years afterward, was one of the most abject feudal slavery. The population of the Valais, on the banks of the Rhine, were in a similar condition. The Bishop of Sion acted the part of a petty king. But still there, as among the Rhætian Alps, civic rights were possessed by townspeople, and a few hardy mountaineers defied in their secluded homes the tyranny of their neighbors.

The castle life of Switzerland, at the period to

which we refer, was no doubt in some cases fruitful in domestic affections. Men were not all savages; the gentle instincts which God has infused into the human breast were not utterly stifled. Even in the bosom of feudalism there were nourished home sympathies; the love of wife and child flowered there. But there were cases in which wild and fitful passions flamed forth with volcanic violence, burning up all the verdure of kindliness and justice; nor were their laws strong enough to check its outbursts, or sanctions sufficiently sacred and powerful to make the transgressor a warning to others. A characteristic story is told of one of the Counts of Tokenburg, illustrative of the lengths of jealousy and revenge to which the feudal lords among the Swiss would, at that period, sometimes go. Count Henry had a beautiful wife, named Ida, who left her wedding-ring by accident close to the open window of her chamber. A raven seized it, carried it off, and dropped it in the neighborhood. It was picked up by a servant, who put it on his hand. His lord, on discovering the ornament on the menial's finger, accused Ida of infidelity; and then, deaf to all explanations which were offered, hurled the unhappy lady from the castle window down among the rocks, and at the same time caused the servant to be bound to the tail of a wild horse to be dragged to death. Ida clung to some bushes and broke her fall; but, refusing to return to the man who had mistrusted and wronged her, she spent the rest of her life in the nunnery of Fischingen.

CHAPTER III.

HEROISM AND INDEPENDENCE.

The nationality which had been nursed in the towns, and which had been fostered by the union between Schwyz, Uri, and Unterwalden, was destined in the fourteenth century to manifest itself in a decided form. On the death of Rudolph of Hapsburgh, Adolph of Nassau succeeded to the imperial crown; but after a short reign, Albert, the son of Rudolph, attained to the same sovereign eminence as his father had reached. To him, therefore, as Emperor of Germany, the free towns of Switzerland and the three confederated forest states were immediately subject; but he soon showed himself an enemy to the former, and wished to change the relation of the latter. His object was to make them dependent upon him and his house, as Dukes of Austria, and thus render them a part of his family possessions. This was contemplated by the cities with just apprehension. Zurich concluded an alliance with neighboring bishops and nobles against Albert. Berne, Fribourg, and Soleure adopted a similar course. The forest people, suspicious of his designs, and prizing their present liberties, objected to become Austrian subjects, and prayed to be left in the condition of their fathers; pleading in support of their claim an express charter from the emperor, Henry VII., by which they were acknowledged as freemen, owing no allegiance but to the emperor. The purpose of Albert evidently was to crush the nascent spirit of freedom and nationality, and to put all Switzerland under his yoke; but he signally failed. The banks of the lake of the four cantons became witnesses of a heroism which baffled the tyrant, and laid the foundation for the subsequent independence of the whole country. In furtherance of his despotic plans, Albert sent two hard-hearted men, named Gessler and Beringer—such is the current story—to levy tolls, exact dues, and punish with severity any signs of insubjection among the people. This task was fulfilled with the utmost rigor, and many a tale is handed down of their pride and oppression. "Is it to be endured," asked Gessler, as he looked at the new-built house of one Stauffacher, "that clownish peasants should erect such handsome dwellings?" Arnold of Melchthal committed a trivial offense; a servant of Beringer seized on his oxen, remarking, as he unyoked them, that "boors might draw their own plows." The Swiss farmer's son struck the man a blow, which broke two of his fingers. Albert's deputy sentenced the father to lose his eyes.

It was not likely that such people as these foresters were—bold, free, and patriotic—should quietly submit to be so trodden down. The wife of Stauffacher is said to have asked her husband, "How long shall arrogance triumph, and humility weep? Shall foreigners become masters of the land, and heirs to our property? What avails it that our mountains are inhabited by men? Are we mothers to suckle sons doomed to become beggars, and bring up our daughters as slaves to foreigners? This cannot be!" Stauffacher, roused by such appeals, went and consulted with Arnold and another patriot, Walter Furst. These three talked together about the state of the country, and the oppression of the duke's agents, and resolved to take steps for the emancipation of their families and neighbors. In the day they sounded the peasants as to their feelings toward the tyrants; and at night they met for conference in a little meadow by the side of the lake, bearing still the name of Rutli—a name derived from the uprooting and clearing of the trees on that verdant slope. Encouraged by the sympathy of friends, they went on Martinmas eve, 1307, each taking ten confederates, to the accustomed trysting-place, and then, lifting up their hands toward the silent stars, shining down from a clear sky on meadow, lake, and hill, they swore to live and die for the freedom of their native home; to resist the oppression of the house of Hapsburgh, but not to inflict on it any wrong; to expel the domineering officers, Gessler and Beringer, but not to cast off allegiance to the empire.

In connection with all this occurs the famous episode of William Tell. He was a cross-bowman of the village of Barglen, and one of the men who had been at Rutli. Gessler, among other expedients for humbling the refractory peasants, set up in the market-place of Altorf a pole with Duke Albert's hat fixed on the top, to which all passers-by were to make obeisance. This act of homage Tell refused to render. He was, therefore, seized and taken before the governor, who immediately pronounced sentence on him for his offense, in the following manner:—"Know, audacious bowman, that thy own art shall serve to punish thee. Thou must shoot from off thy own son's head an apple: take thy aim and miss it not." The boy was bound—as patient as his father was brave—the expert archer bent his bow and exactly shot his mark. "Why hast thou brought a second arrow?" asked Gessler, as he saw him concealing an additional shaft. "If the first had missed the apple," was his reply, "the second should not have missed thy heart." For this Gessler made Tell prisoner, loaded him with chains, and embarked with him on board his boat to carry him over the lake to the Castle of Kussnacht. But a storm arose, and the party were in danger; when, to save his own life, Gessler ordered Tell, who was as expert at the oar as he was in archery, to be unchained, and then committed to him the management of the imperiled bark. Availing himself of this opportunity, the hero guided the boat to shore, and springing out among the rocks, made his escape over the Axenberg, leaving his oppressor to battle as he could with the elements. Afterward, concealing himself in a lane which led to Gessler's castle, Tell shot his oppressor in the heart. This was a wild and cruel outbreak of revenge; but the measures, calmly concerted and carried out in unison by the confederates, were of another description. Early on new year's morning, 1308, a young man, one of the Rutli band, scaled the window of the Austrian castle of Rossberg, in Oberwalden, by the aid of a rope let down by his betrothed, who was living there. He soon introduced twenty companions into the fortress, and made himself master of the place. The same day a party marched to Landenberg, where Beringer lived, and met him on his way to mass. Offering him a new year's present, they were admitted within the castle gates; when, fixing pike heads on the apparently peaceful staves they carried in their hands, as harmless wayfarers might do, they sounded their signal horns according to a preconcerted plan, upon which thirty associates lying in ambush just by sprang up at once to their aid, and the Austrian stronghold was easily captured. No blood was spilt. Beringer and his servants had their lives spared, on the simple condition that they should leave the country forever. The people of Schwyz and of Uri simultaneously demolished the Castles of Schwanau and Kussnacht, and in twenty-four hours the whole work was done, and the cantons were freed entirely from the rod of the oppressor.

We have related these stories according to the traditions of the country, as told in a dramatic, but abbreviated form by Heinrich Zschokke. They are oft related on the banks of the lake. The child in the châlet listens to them with wonder. The figures of the heroes are painted on the walls of houses and churches; mementoes of the men and their deeds abound in the neighborhood. They are commemorated in the simple songs of the people, and in the religious rites of the Church. They have also formed an inspiring theme for the poets of other lands. How much the lapse of time and the activity of imagination may have added to the original incidents of the liberation of Switzerland, it is impossible now to determine; but that there were persons of the names recorded, and performing substantially the exploits ascribed to them, we have not the slightest doubt. The story of Tell in particular has been subject to severe historical criticism, and more than doubt has been thrown by some historians on the cherished traditions connected with his name. In the Wilkina Saga of Saxo Grammaticus, a similar exploit to that of Tell is related of a Danish King Harold; moreover, it is stated that in old documents, published by Kopp, at Lucerne, the name of Gessler is not found in the list of bailiffs residing in the Castle of Kussnacht. The coincidence between the Saga and Swiss traditions is certainly very remarkable; but when it is remembered that the ignorant people of the forest cantons could hardly be acquainted with Danish legends, and that the work of Saxo Grammaticus was first printed and published in 1486, it is difficult to conceive how the Swiss story could be an imitation of the

Danish one. Nor can the negative objection about Gessler's name weigh very much against the ancient tradition of Tell and his heroism. The existence of the patriot is demonstrated by the circumstance, that one hundred and fourteen persons who had known him very well were present at Uri in 1388. Chronicles composed in the next century record his history, and the constant veneration in which he has been held is apparent in an annual solemnity to his honor, celebrated ever since the year 1387.*

Soon after these occurrences, Albert was assassinated by his nephew; and the men of the three cantons, thus relieved from any renewal of his oppression, employed their time in consolidating their union. But Leopold, the son of Albert, succeeding to the possessions of the house of Austria, inherited with them his father's desire to

* Planta observes, vol. i, p. 249, "that Tell's male issue became extinct in 1684, and the female not before 1720. No honors and rewards," he adds, "were conferred on him or his progeny, nor indeed on any of those who on this occasion freed their country. All their descendants lived in obscurity; some are even said to have died in hospitals." It may be noticed, that though Planta, following the German historian Müller, receives the story of Tell as generally authentic, he omits, like his great authority, the anecdote of the apple.

subdue the spirit of the forest league, and accordingly soon led his soldiers against the brave peasants. The proud enemy marched in great force, and carried ropes to hang the Swiss chieftains, so sure they deemed the victory. On the 15th of November, 1315, at the dawn of day, the Austrians approached the scene of conflict. "The helmets and cuirasses of the knights gleamed in the sunshine; as far as the eye could reach, glittered the spears of the first army which had ever been drawn out against the forest cantons, and the Swiss may be supposed to have contemplated so novel a phenomenon with emotion. The narrow way between the ridge of Morgarten and the lake was soon crowded with the close column of horsemen." Pieces of rock and trunks of trees were hurled down on the invaders, which frightened their horses, and threw the ranks into disorder. The Swiss, taking advantage of the confusion, rushed down the hills and struck the foe with halberds and clubs, slaying great numbers, and making a total rout of the rest. By nine o'clock the battle was over, and the cantons were left undisputed masters of the field. The next day a second victory was gained over the Count of Strasburg.

Only temporary unions had hitherto been formed among these warlike foresters; they now resolved on a formal and permanent confederation; and on the 13th of December, 1315, at Brunnen, they began a league which constituted the grand corner-stone of Swiss nationality. Luzern, at first an ally of Austria against its neighbors, afterward joined this famous league, and plighted faith with the other states as a common nation. This brought down on the citizens the wrath of Austria, in which the nobles of the place strongly sympathized, and a plot was formed by them to murder the patriots in their beds, and deliver up the town to Leopold. But a boy overheard the conspirators, and though detected in his discovery, he was allowed to escape, on giving a solemn promise that he would tell nobody of the circumstance. The youth, anxious to save his friends and the rest of the townspeople, yet keeping, as he thought, his promise to the letter, began to speak aloud to a stove in the room where a number of citizens were assembled, stating that he had solemnly sworn to relate to no one what had recently been said in his presence. This led to the deliverance of Luzern from the impending danger. The conspirators were banished; a city council was formed of three hundred burghers, and the independence of the whole community secured.

The league of the Waldstatter, or Forest Cantons, naturally sympathized with other parties in Helvetia who were independent, or were struggling to become so. When the Bernese were attacked, in 1339, by the Emperor Louis, they sent nine hundred soldiers to their help. These warriors took a prominent part in the battle of Laupen, another of the conflicts belonging to the heroic age of Switzerland. They rolled down before them a line of cars armed with scythes, so constructed that they could not be wheeled backward, and when they came within reach of the enemy's line they threw from their slings (in the use of which they were very expert) a shower of stones, which created confusion among the horses. The Swiss then feigned to retire toward the hill in their rear, and the princes pushed forward their cavalry; but the cars opposing their passage, broke their ranks, and the Swiss rushing forward, fought man to man against them. This, like the battle at Morgarten, was soon over; an hour and a half sufficed for the valor of the Bernese and their allies to discomfit completely the army of their enemies. Rudolph d'Erlach, the conquering commander at Laupen, retired, like another Cincinnatus, when the battle was over, to his patrimonial fields, without desiring any reward for his valor.

We have not space minutely to detail the circumstances connected with the further growth of the original Swiss confederation. To the four cantons already united, Schwyz, Uri, Unterwalden, and Luzern, Zurich was added in 1351, Glarus the same year, Zug and Berne the year following. This limited combination of town and forest in the assertion and defense of national independence, "constituted for more than a century the whole federative republic of the Swiss; and even after the accession of other cantons, they retained, together with the title of the eight old cantons, a superiority over the younger members of the league."—*Vieusseux.*

The peace of the inhabitants on the banks of the Aar and Limmat was strangely disturbed in 1375 by the devastating inroads of a band of adventurers, English and French, who were defeated by the Bernese; but a more memorable conflict, not only on account of its political importance to the Swiss, but for an instance of devoted patriotism which it exhibited, was the battle of Sempach, in 1386. Duke Leopold of Austria, full of revenge for the resistance made by the forest cantons to the designs of his house, and supported by neighboring nobles, jealous of the spirit of freedom, which they saw had become so strong, came down with a large army and in much chivalrous pomp to chastise the peasant patriots.

They approached Sempach, a small town in the canton of Luzern, included in the confederacy, bringing with them, as had been done on a former occasion, an abundant provision of ropes for hanging the people. The Austrian army consisted of four thousand picked men. The confederation, on the other hand, could not muster more than one thousand three hundred badly accoutered soldiers. It was a hot day in harvest, and after a short prayer, as they knelt prostrate on the earth, the Swiss rushed upon the formidable phalanx of the enemy, but not with force sufficient to make an impression. A wall of shields, a forest of spears, were before them. The brave defenders of their country fell one after another at the feet of the foe, when Anthony du Port exclaimed, "Strike the poles of the spears, for they are hollow." The spears thus broken, however, were speedily replaced by others; when Arnold of Winkleried, with better success, after exclaiming, "Provide for my wife and children," gathered within his arms the points of the enemy's pikes and plunged them in his bosom, thereby opening a passage into the midst of the Austrian ranks. His companions, fired by his example, pressed on, and soon the flower of the army lay bleeding on the ground, or, panic-struck, took to flight. The victory thus gained by the Swiss, along with another soon after won at Nafels, was decisive, and a period of repose followed, unbroken by the incursions of their old enemies. Certain laws were afterward framed at Sempach to regulate their warfare, and these are strongly illustrative of the character of the people. They pledged themselves not to attack or injure any church unless it was used as a garrison; not to insult any females; not to withhold property or life for their country's good; not to abandon their post even when wounded; not to straggle for plunder, or individually appropriate booty, but to protect and guard such as brought provisions; not to undertake war but by the consent of all the eight cantons, and not to injure one another either in peace or war. War is a dreadful thing even when defensive; but it is to the honor of the Swiss, that in a martial age, with which they were by no means out of sympathy, they did, notwithstanding, endeavor to mitigate its horrors.

The spirit of freedom and independence grew and increased after the battles of Sempach and Nafels, and better methods than fighting were employed to augment the power and influence of the cantons. Zurich, Berne, and Soleure, purchased estates and jurisdictions of the feudal nobility; and the inhabitants of Frutigen, according to an old song quoted by Müller, engaged not to eat beef for seven years, in order to free themselves and their descendants from feudal burdens. Luzern obtained for three thousand gold florins, the cession from the Duke of Austria of his seignorial rights over the Entlibuch; and for a further sum secured the transfer to themselves of other districts. The emperors subsequently favored the confederacy, and renounced whatever remained of imperial jurisdiction. The independence of Appenzell was recognized in 1408, but it did not become a confederated canton till 1513. Soleure and Fribourg were admitted in 1481; Basle and Schaffhausen in 1513. These completed the number of thirteen cantons, with which we find associated, at the commencement of the sixteenth century, in the character of allies, the cities of St. Gall, Mulhausen, and Bienne, Geneva, Neuchâtel, the Grison or Gray League, established by the men of Rhætia and the Valais, who had thrown off the yoke of the old lords of Raron.

War, on the part of Austria, was renewed in 1443 and in 1452; after which another powerful enemy of the Swiss appears in Charles the Bold, Duke of Burgundy. Incensed especially against the cities of Berne and Soleure, this reckless soldier crossed the Jura mountains and attacked the town of Granson, which the confederates had garrisoned, and then he cruelly put to death all the soldiers in the place. The battle of Granson immediately followed, when, after the advanced guard of the Bernese and of Schwyz had commenced the attack, the horns of Uri and Unterwalden were heard sounding a charge, and the banners of Zurich and Schaffhausen were seen waving in the air. "They are the men before whom Austria has fled," cried the Baron of Steur. "Woe to us then," replied Charles; "a handful of men has kept us at bay till now; what will become of us when the rest join them?" The Burgundians were driven from the field "like a herd of cattle," says one who was present, and a camp full of money and luxuries was left a prey to the victors. The more bloody battle of Morat followed, when Charles's army was utterly routed —a prelude to his own miserable death at the siege of Nancy.

But though we have seen the forest cantons and the towns fighting side by side in defense of their common liberties and country, it must not be supposed that perfect amity reigned among them. There were many manifestations of heartburning and jealousy. The town cantons were *aristocratic*, the cities governing the districts around them; the forests cantons were pure *democracies*, all the people within their borders having equal political rights. At a congress held in the town of Stanz, in 1481, the mutual jealousy of the two classes burst out into a flame, which threatened very serious consequences. It was on the occasion of the admission of Fribourg and Soleure being proposed. The mountaineers strongly objected to the increase of the number of aristocratic powers in the Helvetic confederacy, and the opposite party became equally violent. The priest of Stanz went and fetched a hermit called Nicolas Von Flue, who was in great repute among the people of the forest for his ascetic habits, to come and use his influence to restore harmony. The old man, pale and emaciated with fasting, but tall and of a benignant expression of countenance, produced a great effect by his very appearance, as he entered with solemn step like a specter within the hall of council. "You towns," said the peace-maker, "renounce partial alliances among yourselves, which excite the jealousy and suspicion of your elder confederates; and you, people of the Waldstatter, remember the days in which Fribourg and Soleure fought by your side, and receive them in your common bond of alliance. But, confederates all, do not widen too much the hedge which incloses you; do not mix in foreign quarrels; do not listen to intrigue, or accept the price of bribery and treachery against your common land." This simple, pathetic appeal, backed by the old man's venerable aspect and reputation for asceticism, produced the desired result. All differences were at once settled, some additions were made to the articles of confederacy, and the bells of the churches from the Jura to the Alps soon after rang peals of joy at the preservation of peace.

Besides dissensions, which, though allayed, were not extinguished at the Congress of Stanz, intestine commotion was not uncommon in the towns, and in particular may be mentioned a tragical occurrence of that nature in the year 1484. John Waldmann, a peasant's son of the Zug canton, rose to great eminence and power in the city of Zurich, having distinguished himself by his talents and courage, especially by his exploits in the battles of Morat and Nancy. Waldmann, in his office of burgomaster, was charged with despotic conduct and an abuse of his influence, and the country people rose in arms against him. Mediation was attempted; but Waldmann, venturing on his authority, which he thought was well established, pursued his own course, and to guard against his enemies slept in the town hall. The vengeance of the people at length burst out, and the burgomaster and his adherents were put to the rack and afterward beheaded. Other outrages were committed in different parts by individuals, and in three months of the year 1480 no less than one thousand five hundred assassins and robbers were sentenced to death—a fact which shows how many desperate characters there were in a nation celebrated for its simple manners, its patriotism, and its bravery. But another foul blot attaching, not merely to individuals, but to the general policy and character of the confederates, is found in the engagement of their soldiers as mercenaries in foreign wars—a practice which began in the fifteenth century. Men enlisted with the sanction of the cantons in the service of other countries, without caring for the question at issue between the belligerent parties, but simply looking for pay, or influenced by a wild love of adventure and strife. Over the Jura into France, and over the Alps into Italy, did the youths of the forest and city go forth from their homes, in armor marked with a white cross, and wearing felt hats surmounted with a feather, to sell their lives for money or for the gratification of martial passion. Some have attempted to defend this practice of the Swiss, and we regret to find so excellent a historian as Planta engaged on that side. Far more in accordance with our views are the remarks of Grattan: "It is impossible to trace, without a feeling of repugnance, the relations, whether foreign or domestic, in which Switzerland was engaged during a period which, in spite of martial achievements, must be deemed the most deplorable and disgraceful of her history. It became the only object of state policy in Switzerland to drive a lucrative traffic with the blood of its inhabitants; and though the article must be acknowledged to have fetched a price, it is not the less a scandalous blot in the history of the country that so vile a trade should so long have remained the only one pursued with any energy by the people and its leaders. It is true that the Helvetic seats of government were surrounded with more splendor than ever. Embassadors crowded thither from the emperor and the pope, and from many other monarchs, princes, nobles, and free towns, soliciting with emulous zeal their friendship and alliance, and bidding against each other for the iron arm of Switzerland, by offers of absolution, special privileges, rich presents, large pensions, and high pay." Trying the question not on the principles of expediency, or according to the manners and practices of that or any other age, but by the everlasting laws of moral rectitude, not a word can be said in defense of the conduct of the Swiss in their mercenary services. Immoral consequences, in addition to the immorality of the system itself, followed to the sore distress of the true Swiss patriots; and Bullinger, at a subsequent period, records "that a lewd and wanton life was commonly practiced, with gluttony, gaming, dancing, and all manner of wantonness, day and night, especially where diets were held, as at Zurich, Luzern, and Baden:* (the latter, it may be observed, was a most licentious place.) The common people in town and country were drawn away from honest labor to idleness, lewdness, and warlike undertakings, and reckless and abandoned habits thus prevailed everywhere."

CHAPTER IV.

THE REFORMATION.

THE errors, superstitions, and immoralities of the Church of Rome had become so gross and startling in the Swiss branch of that communion at the early part of the sixteenth century, that it only needed some bold and resolute spirit, under the blessing of God, to place them in their true light, and to oppose them by the pure religion of the Bible, to produce a reaction in the minds of

* This is Baden near Zurich, and must not be confounded with any of the Badens in Germany. Baden simply means Baths.

the people, and to lay the foundation of a grand religious reform. A farmer's son, brought up amid the scenery of the Toggenburg, full of those aspirations after freedom which mountain scenes seem to kindle and mountain breezes to fan—a youth of energy, of studious habits, of large knowledge for the times in which he lived, of a strong will, of a warm heart, resolute in action, eloquent in speech, was the instrument chosen by Divine Providence for the purpose. Ulrich Zwingle, the individual referred to, whose youth had then ripened into mature manhood, appeared, in 1516, as a preacher at Einsiedlen, (at that period, as it is still, a famous and influential monastery,) and afterward at Zurich, in both which places his ministry evinced that he had been taught by the Scriptures to grasp and feel those great principles of evangelical truth which are the most formidable antagonists of papal corruptions. Through his own experience, under the teaching of divine grace, he had learned that simple faith in the glorious work of the one Mediator, a hearty dependence on the sacrifice and intercession of Christ alone, could convey to the soul a peace, an assurance, and a joy, which trust in the prayers of the Virgin and saints, or the performance of multiplied ceremonies, or the presumptuous words of absolution from priestly lips, could never bring.

Zwingle had not merely, as a student of scientific theology, discovered that certain dogmas were unsound, and that contrary ones were scriptural; but he had received from God a new spiritual life which could find its nourishment only in the faith of Christ as revealed in the New Testament. For the mind to be diverted from Him, the only hope of the sinner, to other and vain grounds of dependence—for access to Him, the only Mediator, to be hindered by the introduction of subordinate mediators, Zwingle, taught by the ever-present Comforter of the Church, plainly saw was fatal to all evangelical tranquillity of mind. At the same time he also discerned that simple reliance upon the one Saviour and Lord of the Church was the most powerful impulse to a life of practical holiness. The preaching of this very remarkable man and illustrious reformer in the old cathedral of Zurich gathered together vast crowds, who listened eagerly to a voice which proclaimed with marvelous freshness, sympathy, and power, the way of life as taught in the gospel, and which, with sincere and earnest love, invited the sinner to place his hope on the Lamb of God.

The sale of indulgences was one of the most obvious scandals of the age. What Tetzel did in Germany, a friar named Samson was doing in Switzerland. From canton to canton this ignorant hireling traveled in the prosecution of his infamous trade, uttering extravagances enough to revolt even the confirmed papist. The doctrine of indulgences, as taught by the highest authorities of the papal Church, does not, it is contended, set aside the necessity of repentance; but certainly Samson made the papers he sold do everything for the sinner, and moreover in the grossest way he showed that all he thought of was the filling of the Church's coffers. "Let those pass first who have money," cried this miserable creature; "we shall afterward listen to the poor." At Baden, not far from Zurich, he went round the church-yard singing the service for the dead, and crying out, *Ecce volant*, "See they fly;" pretending that by the indulgences which the people bought, the souls of their friends were escaping from purgatory and flying up to heaven. The seller of these wares could not succeed at Zurich in the face of Zwingle's opposition. The work of reform went on there under the leadership of this holy and apostolic man. Other honest-hearted laborers in the same cause, like-minded with himself, whose eyes God's truth had opened, whose hearts God's love had touched—Ecolampadius, Bullinger, and Haller, especially—strengthened his hands and helped on his success. Both at Berne and Basle the principles of the

Reformation took root, and the worship of images was abolished, but not without some violent measures, in which rashness of zeal got the better of sound judgment and Christian consistency. In the progress of the work, an important conference was held at Berne, in 1528. Zwingle, with a deputation from Zurich, was present. Glarus, Appenzel, Basle, Schaffhausen, St. Gall, Bienne, Lausanne, and the Grisons, also sent representatives. It was determined by the assembly that no argument would be admitted which was not grounded on a text of Scripture, to the exclusion of other authorities—a mode of deciding the grand questions in dispute fatal of course to the success of the Roman theologians, while it showed the preponderance of Protestant influence. This meeting was a decisive step in the right direction, and produced a powerful effect in favor of the reformed cause; but the opposition made by the Lutherans to the Zwinglians (as the Swiss reformers were called) on the question of the nature of the Lord's Supper—Luther maintaining the doctrine of consubstantiation, and Zwingle holding that it was a simple ordinance of commemoration, fellowship, and love—tended much to hinder the advance of the Swiss reformation by the disunion it exhibited to the opponents of Rome, and much more by the violent passions it aroused in the breasts of the Protestant controversialists. The conduct of the Anabaptists, full of fanatical excess, having no connection with the leading tenet which gave them their name, but rather the outbursts of a species of religious madness, also operated in a way most unfriendly to the great ecclesiastical movement, with which, though perfectly separate in point of principle and spirit, the advocates of Rome strove to represent it as intimately connected, and, indeed, as one of its natural outgrowths.

In addition to argument, misrepresentation, and abuse, force was employed by the papal party, when it had the power, in resisting the reformation. Jacob Keyser, a minister of the Zurich canton, was burned publicly at Schwytz, in May, 1529; the martyr, in the midst of the flames, invoking the name of the Lord Jesus as his only solace and helper in the fiery trial. Farel at Orbe, was assaulted by the mob, who would have most likely killed him if the Bernese bailiff had not come to his rescue. At Soleure, a number of Romanists gathered about a house where the Protestants were worshiping, and pointed a field-piece at the inmates, which would have done dreadful execution among them, had it not been for the noble firmness of the avoyer, who placed himself at the mouth of the cannon, exclaiming:

"If you are determined to shed the blood of your fellow-citizens, you shall begin with mine." The amount of sanguinary persecution in Switzerland was very little, compared with what obtained in some other countries, but this was owing to the preponderating number of Protestants in certain of the cantons, and their political relations to the rest.

The persecutions by the Roman Catholics excited the anger of Zurich, and a proclamation of war was the result. Assisted by Berne, St. Gall, Mulhausen, and Bienne, the Zurichers advanced toward Schwyz to chastise their brethren of the mountain and forest for their inhuman treatment of Keyser, and their sympathy in persecuting principles. But John Oebly, the landamman of Glarus, who had already saved his own canton from the horrors of a civil war, now appeared in the field as an angel of peace, and by his prudent and zealous interference extinguished for a time the torch of strife. A conference ensued; a truce was proclaimed; the soldiers on both sides began to mingle as friends, and a *religious* peace, as it was called, was concluded in June, 1529. "You Swiss," cried a deputy of Strasburgh, "are a strange people; for although you seem divided, you are still united, and do not forget your ancient alliances."

After the settlement at the Synod of Berne, in 1532, of the Helvetic confession of faith, (a thoroughly evangelical standard of doctrine, and one in full harmony with those published by the reformed Churches of France and Holland, as well as with that of the Scottish kirk,) and after the full concession of liberty of conscience by the Protestant cantons, the parties who retained an affection for the see of Rome, its doctrines and ceremonies, were more than ever dissatisfied with the condition of religious affairs in Switzerland, and were ready to avail themselves of any occasion to take up arms against their brethren of opposite sentiments, hoping to crush by force what could not be subdued by reason and persuasion. The senate of Zurich, besides adopting some questionable measures in reference to St. Gall, endeavored to *force* the papal cantons to allow the free use of the Scriptures by forbidding all commerce with them, going so far as to deny the supplying of salt, an article of traffic of essential importance, which the forest cantons received from Zurich. This measure, which Zwingle opposed as uncharitable, aroused the inhabitants of the Waldstatter to a state of furious indignation, and excited them to cry, "The sword alone can cut this knot." Indeed, not only were there religious reasons for the enmity which had before existed, and now again blazed forth, but political considerations and feelings tended to foment the existing quarrels.

The seat of Protestantism was in the towns; Popery retained its strong-holds in the mountain villages, in the forest cantons especially, where the rites of the ancient faith had become blended with the historical recollections of Tell and his compatriots. Popery seemed to the ignorant people about the lake of the four cantons to be a part of patriotism, and to it they transferred the enthusiasm awakened by the heroic memories of their fatherland. Between town and forest, as we have before seen, there had long existed great jealousies. The aristocratic element of the one was opposed to the democratic element of the other, and at the time of the controversies about the reformation in Switzerland, the old political feeling was revived in conjunction with the religious excitement. Zurich and the city cantons, on the one side, were political, no less than ecclesiastical antagonists of Schwyz; Unterwalden, and the rest on the other side. The Romanists prepared for war this time in earnest; so did the opposite party. The fatal battle of Cappel, that mournful episode in the history of the Swiss reformation, was the result: there Zwingle fell. He attended the Zurich troops in the capacity of chaplain, according to the custom of the age, not without some forebodings, it is said, of the fate awaiting him. The battle went hard with the army on the side of the reformation. It was broken, routed, dispersed; and Zwingle, who went to preach and pray, not to fight, though his presence there at all, according to our better notions of ministerial position and duty, can hardly be considered proper, was struck on the head by a stone, as he was kneeling by the side of a dying man, and administering to him religious consolation. Repeated wounds were inflicted on the reformer, and he lay under a pear-tree by the roadside, with his hands clasped and his eyes lifted up to heaven. There, in the dark night, he was found by the enemy. "Call upon the saints, and confess to our priests," was the cry. Zwingle needed no mediator but the one High Priest who ever liveth to make intercession for us. His silence, when the question about a confessor was put to him, excited suspicion. "No doubt you are one of the heretics," said one. "I think it is Zwingle," cried another. "Zwingle!" exclaimed Feckinger of Unterwalden, "that vile heretic!—then die;" plunging his sword at the same instant into the reformer's throat. Zwingle had said, as he lay bleeding, "They may kill the body, they cannot kill the soul;" he now experienced the truth of those blessed words; while every indignity was shown to his senseless corpse, which the enemy afterward burned to ashes. Tidings of his death spread a panic over Zurich. His poor weeping wife had listened with anguish to the distant reports of artillery, and her worst fears were fulfilled when the people ran crying through the streets, "Zwingle is fallen!" Son, too, and brother, and son-in-law, had all perished in the strife. It was a mournful day indeed for the reformer's family, and for the whole city. The preacher, the shepherd, the adviser, was gone. "These men may fall upon his body," said his friends; "they may kindle their piles and brand his innocent life, but he lives; this invincible hero lives in eternity, and leaves behind him an immortal monument of glory which no flames can destroy. God, for whose honor he had labored even at the price of his blood, will make his memory eternal." Every one who has crossed the Albis from Zurich to Zug must have paused to notice the stone monument by the wayside at Cappel, where Zwingle fell. It marks the site of the pear-tree where he lay and bled; and as one looks over the now quiet scene on a summer's day, and dwells upon the calm majesty of the mountains in the neighborhood, what a type it seems of the character of the man, and of the celestial tranquillity of his spirit, now that all the storms and battles of this world have for him been long over, and he lives in the sunshine of his Lord's favor and love.

The Protestants rallied after the battle of Cappel, but only to sustain a second defeat. Victorious in debate, they failed in their appeal to arms, as if God intended to teach them that the proper weapons of their warfare were not carnal. But the Roman Catholics were wearied at last with fighting, and were glad to come to terms of peace; whereupon it was agreed that the five Catholic cantons should be left unmolested in the possession of their religion, and that the Protestant cantons should be the same.

In Geneva, where ecclesiastical influence had been very powerful—the city being under the government of a bishop, who was a temporal prince—the Reformation made its way, in a great measure, through the indefatigable labors of the famous Farel. The alliance of the Bernese materially helped on the cause in its outward and political aspects. The citizens who had adopted the Protestant faith overturned the altars, destroyed the images, and excommunicated the bishops. Then mass was forbidden, and the intolerance of Rome, alas! was copied to some degree by those who protested against it. In Lausanne, too, where the people had seen enough in the conduct of the priests to disgust them with Popery, the Reformation obtained now a signal triumph. All sorts of immoralities had prevailed among the priesthood, and it had not been an uncommon thing for ecclesiastics in that city to fight in the church, and to walk through the streets at night in military dresses and with naked swords. When a theological discussion was to take place in Lausanne, under the leadership of Farel, the Roman Catholics declined to meet him, and in the end there was an abolition of the mass and the appointment of reformed clergymen to the various parishes.

A more illustrious man, in point of learning and extensive influence, than any we have mentioned in our notice of the Swiss reformation, was John Calvin, and with Geneva in particular his name and memory are associated. He visited the city when young, and thus became acquainted with Farel, whose opinions and sentiments accorded with his own. They attached great importance to the doctrine of divine predestination, desired the abolition of all festivals except the Sunday, used leavened bread in the sacrament, recognized a spiritual presence of Christ in the bread and wine, and enforced the moral duties of life with the greatest strictness. Some of their peculiarities offended even their Protestant brethren, and in consequence of their refusing to submit to the decisions of a synod held at Lausanne, Calvin and Farel were forbidden by the magistrates of Geneva to remain in the town. But though exiled for a while, Calvin was earnestly requested at length to return to his former post. "Perceiving the necessity of having a moral censorship, in order to restrain the utter licentiousness which threatened the very existence of the community, he proposed to establish a consistory to act as *censor morum*, composed of the pastors or parish incumbents, two members of the council of state or executive, two members of the council of two hundred, one of the syndics, and a secretary. This and other regulations proposed by Calvin, concerning Church government and discipline, were approved by the general council of all the citizens, and received the form of law in November, 1541. The consistory assembled every Thursday, and Calvin, who always attended the sittings, may be said to have been its presiding spirit. It had very extensive and almost inquisitorial powers; it took cognizance of immoralities, of blasphemies, of profanations, and other offenses against religion. The punishments were fine, imprisonment, and in some cases death. This institution of the consistory has continued to exist down to the present day, though considerably modified. Calvin also undertook the task of collecting and revising the old laws and edicts, so as to form a body of civil law for the republic, which was approved of in 1543 by the council general. At the same time he was not unmindful of the cultivation of the mind; and he proposed and effected the establishment of a public college, called the academy, for teaching the arts and sciences, in which he himself lectured three times a week on theology, and which soon acquired and has ever since maintained a high character among the schools of learning in Europe, and has been a nursery of pastors and divines to the reformed Churches of France and other countries."—*Vieusseux.*

The amount of labor which this indefatigable man accomplished, in spite of his delicate constitution and comparatively short life, (for he died at fifty-five, worn out by toil,) is really amazing. In addition to all his multifarious duties in connection with Geneva, he wrote numerous works, remarkable for their depth of thought, copiousness, and even elegance of diction, besides carrying on a correspondence which embraced within its range the principal reformers of Europe. "Shall I be idle when my Lord comes?" was the answer he gave on his dying bed to those who entreated him to relax his exertions; and it was in the spirit of those noble words that he ever lived and worked. His virtues were of the stern, heroic cast. He was Elijah-like, Luther-like; but was wanting constitutionally in that tenderness of soul and that genial warmth which sometimes adorn and enliven even the severest natures. The part he took in reference to the death of Servetus, is the one stain on his memory. Every Protestant must deplore it as utterly inconsistent with that spirit of tolerance which is a part of his religion. Consistent vindicators of Calvin in this matter, among men who love the reformation as preparing liberty for every man in his religious profession, there cannot be; but historic justice demands of us to remember that Calvin only imbibed the spirit of former days, which in his time still cast their shadows over the Churches; that he did what many of his brethren approved; and especially it should be observed that Roman Catholics, who are very apt to malign the name of the reformer on account of this single fact in his life, are the last people in the world who should do so, seeing that he only committed on a small scale what the authorities of their Church have perpetrated on a very large one, and what they have continued to do, notwithstanding the advance of knowledge and civilization.

Calvin died in 1564, and was succeeded in the

pastoral office by Theodore Beza. A glimpse of the latter when he had grown very old, and after the cause to which his life was devoted had been periled by war, must close this chapter. Political relations and disputes were mixed up with the vicissitudes of the Reformation in Geneva as elsewhere. After peace had been for many years maintained between that city and Savoy, Charles Emanuel, its duke, who had driven away the Protestant ministers from Chablais in his own dominions, made an assault on Geneva, which, if successful, would have been, no doubt, of serious consequence to the interests of the reformed religion. A small body of his troops, on a December night in 1602, scaled the walls of Geneva, intending to give a signal to their comrades to force the gates; but a sentry, hearing the noise, gave an alarm and roused the citizens, who barricaded the streets, while the guard let down the portcullis and swept away the scaling ladders. The Savoyards who had entered the city were hurled into the ditch, or killed, and those who remained outside retreated. Old Beza was quietly sleeping in his bed during this stormy and critical night, little dreaming of the danger impending over the city. The good man, owing to his infirmities, had ceased to preach; but when he heard of what had happened he hastened to the church, and summoned the citizens to join him in singing the hundred and twenty-fourth Psalm, which has continued every year on the anniversary of the event to be chanted by the Genevese, in devout commemoration of God's goodness to their fathers. The Psalm seemed as if it were written for the occasion, and how often are minds familiar with the Bible astonished at the pertinency of these sacred Hebrew compositions to passing events in individual and national history! "If it had not been the Lord who was on our side, now may Israel say; if it had not been the Lord who was on our side, when men rose up against us: then they had swallowed us up quick; when their wrath was kindled against us: then the waters had overwhelmed us, the stream had gone over our soul: then the proud waters had gone over our soul. Blessed be the Lord, who hath not given us as a prey to their teeth. Our soul is escaped as a bird out of the snare of the fowlers: the snare is broken, and we are escaped. Our help is in the name of the Lord, who made heaven and earth."

CHAPTER V.

WARS OF RELIGION.

Such is the title given to those conflicts in Switzerland which form the chief incidents of its history during the seventeenth century. Though a knowledge of the opinions and spirit of the age throughout Europe, and of the previous blending of the religious with the political in all the Swiss cantons, removes surprise from our minds that the great ecclesiastical events of the reformation should have entailed warfare for many years, yet we cannot but lament (useless though such lamentations be) that the hallowed name of religion should have been so dishonored as to be made the occasion of bloodshed and devastation. But it is not superfluous to record the truth which the growing light kindled at the reformation has since taught us—that argument and persuasion, not force in any form, are the weapons which belong to the armory of the Christian faith; that as Christ's kingdom is not of this world, it is forbidden to his servants to fight with earthly weapons for its extension, and that they that thus use the sword shall perish by the sword. There have, however, been periods in history when it has been necessary for a nation to resist, by force of arms, the attempst of invaders or oppressors to exterminate their religion.

Our limited space prevents us from entering into the story of the wars in the Grisons, between Roman Catholics and Protestants, in which, we lament to say, the latter were the aggressors; and from telling the horrible tale of the Catholic revolt in the Vattellina, and of the massacre of the Protestants in cold blood. Nor can we narrate the fruitless attempts of the Duke of Savoy, the King of France, and the Pope of Rome at mediation, the invasion of the Grisons by Austria, and the submission for a time of the former to the latter power.

We must also pass over the conflicts and intrigues of France and Austria, in reference to this little mountain league, so illustrative of the Grison proverb—"Austria *takes*, and France *lies*," —and of the progress and success of the struggle by the mountaineers for the recovery of their independence, acting on the maxim, "Let us trust no foreign power, but seek help only from our arms."

The thirty years' war of Germany only remotely relates to Switzerland, as she was not one of the powers involved in that contest; though many of her sons served as mercenaries in its memorable battles, and the peace of the country was disturbed by bands of adventurers, the refuse of the two great armies. The treaty of Westphalia in 1648, however, was a fact of importance to Switzerland, inasmuch as it acknowledged the independence of the confederation, and its freedom from all claims on the part of the German empire.

The peasants' war, which broke out in 1653, was only a new form of the old Swiss controversy between country and town. The rural inhabitants complained of monopolies enjoyed by the citizens, and of the taxes they imposed on certain necessaries. The insurrection began at Entlibuch, in the canton of Luzern, but soon spread over other districts till half Switzerland was thrown into commotion. The insurgents committed some desperate cruelties; so that whatever might be their original grievances, it was seen that all the friends of order must unite to put down the terrible revolt. Though a war between town and country, it was not like former wars between canton and canton, between one common interest and another, between order and confusion, but between class and class, between peasant and burgess, between agriculture and commerce, between lawless violence and settled government. The Waldstatter, therefore, united with the other states in a determined step to crush the turbulent peasantry Efforts at conciliation were made, but peace was not restored till after two engagements, one of which was very severe.

The first war, commonly called religious, pertained to the period now under review; but the second, if we include the period surveyed in the last chapter, began in 1655. Heart-burnings between the Roman Catholic and Protestant cantons had not been extinguished by the formal friendship which followed the close of the previous war. Nor did the close tie of their confederacy prevent each party from entering into such foreign alliances as it chose. So the one formed treaties with the English and Dutch, the other with the Dukes of Savoy. Elements of discord between them were silently at work, when a case of persecution in the Roman Catholic canton of Schywz aroused the sympathy of Protestant Zurich for the persecuted. Appeals were made to former treaties about toleration: but in vain. So the martial Zurichers, joined by Schaffhausen and Basle, again drew the sword against their old enemies. Berne, too, came to the help of its old friends. A decisive engagement at Willmergen, near Luzern, took place on the 15th of January, 1656, when the Bernese were defeated with great loss, and a treaty of peace ensued, which left the Roman Catholic cantons to do still as they pleased. Nine weeks of war, and half a million of florins, and at least a thousand brave lives, had been spent for nothing. Fifty years of quiet ensued, during which Switzerland became a place of refuge for the persecuted French Protestants under Louis XIV., and the persecuted Waldenses under the Duke of Savoy. The generous practical sympathy of the Protestant cantons at this time toward their suffering brethren from other lands was very beautiful. Large sums were expended on their behalf, and Zurich alone is reported to have contributed four hundred thousand florins.

Of old there had been much quarreling between the Bishop of St. Gall and the people of the Toggenburg. He treated them as vassals, denying them the rights they justly claimed. The majority of them were Protestants, and all such were excluded by him from offices of trust and advantage. The contest between them grew worse and worse—the religious aspects of the disputes became more and more decided. Zurich and the Protestant cantons declared themselves the defenders of these oppressed people; Luzern and the Roman Catholic cantons took part with the abbot. The war which ensued is the second religious war of this period, the third from the beginning. Some Roman Catholic soldiers murdered two harmless men and mutilated a helpless woman. This roused those on the other side to make terrible reprisals. These atrocities, as well as another committed by the people of the abbot, who placed their own general, on account of alleged cowardice, on a miserable horse, and chased him amid savage howlings to a bridge on the Setter, where they shot him, and then cut up his body—show how much of the barbarous spirit of their early ancestors still lingered in some of the Swiss, and how little civilization and religion had done for their character and habits. As many as one hundred and fifty thousand men were under arms in Switzerland, engaged in this which proved to be the last of their civil and religious wars, until their renewal in very recent times. Several actions took place, and the last, which settled the question in dispute, was fought at Willmergen, where the two religious parties had met fifty years before; but now the result was different, for the Bernese broke through the ranks of their foes, and covered the field with two thousand slain, including five Capuchin friars. The Roman Catholics sued for peace, and a treaty was formed at Aargau, giving religious freedom to the inhabitants of the Thurgau and the Rheinthal, and restricting the power of the Abbot of St. Gall over the people of the Toggenburg. The old ecclesiastic obstinately resisted the terms, and died in exile; but his successor agreed to them.

CHAPTER VI.

A LONG PEACE.

Peace continued from 1712 to 1793, a period marked by few incidents, and noticeable chiefly for the opportunities it afforded for the quiet working of those different forms of republican government which, within so small a space, wrought side by side, affording to the philosophical politician an interesting group of subjects for study and speculation.

Berne was the chief of the first division composed of the aristocratic cantons. Its council, self-elected, might amount to two hundred and ninety-nine, but it seldom numbered so many. The only persons eligible were the burghers, descendants of the old families who founded the city, and such as might have since been admitted to that rank. The executive consisted of a senate chosen out of the council. The principal magistrates were two avoyers, two treasurers, and four bannerets. One was called reigning avoyer, and presided over the meetings of the council, and was deemed chief of the republic. A singular appendage to the actual government of Berne was the "exterior state," as it was called—a school, in short, for training up the young patricians, in which the forms and offices of the canton were imitated, and a mock semblance of the doings of their fathers was carried on by the sons from year to year, till they were thus themselves trained to bear the burdens of the state. The Bernese government has been much applauded for its general integrity, notwithstanding that its constitution was of a stationary character, and not subject to the direct influence of the people at large. It had all the faults, says one of its members, but all the virtues of an aristocracy, and the commendation probably is as true as the admission which qualifies it. Peculation was never its crime, nor was it guilty of inquisitorial tyranny. No bribe could seduce its members; in illustration of which M. de Bonstatten, the patrician just alluded to, relates the following circumstance:—"A peasant, who had a suit before our court, left one day, unobserved, a basket full of lump sugar in the kitchen of one of the judges, hoping thus to secure his favor, without committing either the magistrate or himself. The peasant was summoned before the judges, charged with an attempt at bribery, reprimanded, and sent to prison." But this authority adds, that the Italian bailiwicks were by no means so scrupulous. It may be remarked, in addition, that the prison discipline of the Bernese was superior to that in many countries, and obtained the commendation of the great philanthropist, John Howard, when he visited the canton toward the close of the century. The criminals may still be seen at work on the highways, much after the fashion described by the great reformer of the prison world of Europe.

Close aristocracies are sure to awaken suspicion, to lack the enjoyment of public confidence, and to be assailed sooner or later, as the result of dissatisfaction from without. It was so with the aristocratic government of Berne. An officer named Henzi, in 1749, promoted petitions to the legislature for a concession to all the burghers of the right of election. For this he was banished five years, and on his return he engaged in a conspiracy to overturn the executive, and to place the whole administration of affairs on a broader basis. Some of his associates were men of far different character from himself. He was patriotic—they were selfish. He sought his country's welfare—their hearts were set on gain. He wished as far as possible to avoid bloodshed—they were advocates for the most violent measures. On discovering this, Henzi sought to break off the connection and escape, but it was too late. He was tried and executed with two of his accomplices, and others of them were banished. His wife, stung by her loss, as she reached the Rhine with her two boys, exclaimed, "If I knew that these children would not avenge the blood of their father, I should desire, dear as they are to me, to see them ingulfed in these waves." "But her sons," adds Zschokke, "were actuated with nobler sentiments than their mother. One of them, who became governor of the pages in the service of the Stadtholder of the Netherlands, afterward requited, by services rendered to the citizens of his native place, his own unmerited misfortune."

The government of Fribourg was a still more limited aristocracy, being confined to seventy-one families, somewhat like the exclusiveness of Venice with her golden book. Out of the two hundred members of council, a senate and council of secresy were chosen by what was called "blind ballot," being in fact an accidental throw of balls into a box. That compartment which *happened* to get the greatest number decided the election of the candidate whose name was written upon it. Some of the people, dissatisfied with such a strange political constitution, broke out into rebellion in 1781, but were defeated. Other cantons, by persuasion, induced Fribourg to modify some of its peculiarities; but it still retained the most oligarchic government in Switzerland. In Soleure, though the council was confined to the aristocracy, a show of popular rights was allowed by the assembling of all the burghers once a year, to confirm, *pro formâ*, the magistrates in office. Lucern had a more real blending of patrician and plebeian; for though that distinction was not lost sight of, the latter class were eligible to a seat in the senate, and the great council was elected by general suffrage. All questions of war and taxation were, at the same time, submitted to a general assembly of burghers.

"The second class of cantons, the government of which might be called *municipal*, consisted of Zurich, Basle, and Schaffhausen. The feature which mainly distinguished them from the former was that the sovereign power resided among all the burghers of the principal city of each canton, who elected the members of both the great council and of the senate, every burgher being eligible to sit in either." The Zurich burghers were divided into thirteen tribes, one of which, called noble, enjoyed certain privileges above the rest. The burghers of Basle formed eighteen tribes, with no noble or patrician class. Here, too, as in Fribourg, the principle of chance was adopted in elections; but then, instead of a blind ballot, there was a drawing of lots. This practice, strange as it may seem, was adopted even in the choice of professors for the university. Three candidates who had taken a doctor's degree drew lots, and if the successful one did not exactly suit his new office, he changed places with some other professor. Schaffhausen, also, had its tribes, twelve in number, and like the rest derived its revenues from demesnes, tithes, and duties. In both the classes of cantons just noticed, the sovereign power was vested exclusively in the chief town, the smaller towns and the whole country being subject to it. Subordinate local governments, however, existed, and the supreme administration is said to have been generally moderate and liberal toward the dependencies, while the charges of carrying on public affairs were extremely economical.

With regard to the third class of cantons, the Waldstatter, together with Zug, Glarus, and Appenzell, we need only observe that they continued, as from the beginning, purely democratical, every shepherd and peasant having a share in the election of their governors, and also meeting in the *landsgemeinde*, or great assembly, for the decision of all important matters affecting the canton. It must not, however, be supposed that these democracies were as pure in practice as they were in theory. The history of Zug, for example, shows that a family might gain virtually an aristocratic influence, and lord it over other citizens. There we find the family of the Zurlaubens guiding the votes of the people to a large extent, and keeping power in their own hands. In opposition to this family influence, we see Anthony Schumacher busily at work, supplanting the parties of whom he was jealous, and at last in his turn reigning almost supreme. His measures became most arbitrary and cruel, till the public were tired of him and his faction, and sentenced him to the scaffold; a punishment commuted to hard labor, in the endurance of which he soon died. Foreign politics and alliances were mixed up with internal disputes. One party at Zug favored Austria, the other France; and they were called respectively the *hard* and the *mild*. The working of the system of foreign enlistment also stands connected with the troubles at Zug. Enlistments in the French army had been encouraged, for which subsidies were paid and money also privately distributed. People thus became corrupted by bribes from a foreign power to maintain a line of policy which it approved—a state of things fatal to patriotism and national integrity, and most pernicious to the cultivation of social virtue in general.

The other cantons stood in relation of allies to the foregoing. They were the Grisons, the Valais, St. Gall, Bienne, Neuchâtel, Grison, Engelberg, and Geneva. Among the Grisons, democracy was maintained to the fullest possible extent, so that the small Alpine region over which the bond of the Gray League extended was broken up into no less than sixty minute districts, each in fact containing a distinct republic with full powers of self-government. These sent deputies to the meeting of the Grison confederation, which was held in annual succession at Coire, Davos, and Ilantz. But even here, with an almost infinitesimal division of power, human tendencies had their way, and a few persons obtained the management of all the rest. The Valais had ten districts, of which the seven of the Upper Valais were masters of the three Lower Valais. Six of the districts were democracies, the rest had some aristocratic element; and one, that of Sion, was subject to the bishop, who possessed, however, but very limited sovereign rights. St. Gall was a double state—one part under the dominion of the abbot, whose sway in the eighteenth century was somewhat short of the absolutism it formerly possessed; and the other, the city, in fact, was a combination of aristocratic and popular rule. Singularly enough, the abbey stood in the midst of the city, and the territories of the abbey surrounded the city; so that the municipality was a sort of ring inserted in the middle of and cutting in two the prelatical domain. The town of Bienne had its council, court of justice, and mayor, and managed its own affairs; but was dependent, in some small degree, on Basle. Neuchâtel became part of the dominion of the House of Brandenburg in 1707 by its own vote, and thus was incorporated in the kingdom of Prussia. Its relations to the government of that country were too complicated and unimportant to be noticed here. Grison, the smallest democracy in the world, consisting only of a thousand people, and Engelberg, subject to a bishop, require no particular notice; and indeed of some others it may be said, as of these, that they offer no observation which may tend to illustrate the spirit and genius of this heterogeneous commonwealth. Geneva was full of political disturbances in the eighteenth century, class being arrayed against class, democracy fighting with aristocracy; the whole being of small importance, and reminding one, as the Emperor Paul used to say, of tempests in a tumbler of water. "The government of Geneva, as settled by the pacification of 1768, consisted of a great council, a senate, and a general assembly. All laws were proposed by the senate, discussed in the great council, and then laid before the assembly of the citizens, who approved of them or rejected them by majority of suffrages, but without discussion. The senate had the executive power, administered the finances, and exercised the privilege of conferring, under certain conditions, the rights of burghership, which was rendered more accessible than before. The principal magistrates, such as the four syndics, were chosen from among the senators. The senate also appointed to one-half of the vacancies in the great council, who in their turn filled up vacancies in the senate. The general assembly approved or rejected the proposed laws, imposed taxes, declared war or peace, and contracted alliances."

With regard to the bond between the cantons themselves, and between them and their allies, we can only observe that it was far less intimate than that which once connected the Dutch provinces, or than what now obtains between the American States. The Helvetic confederacy had neither central government nor a permanent magistrate-in-chief. The executive was vested in each canton, and such general legislation as there might be in the federal council was, according to specific instructions, given to the members by those whom they represented. The meetings of the federal council were ordinary and extraordinary—the former being annually held at Baden till 1712, and afterward at Frauenfeld; the latter being moveable according to circumstances. Zurich took a certain precedence of the rest, its deputy being president of the federal assembly, and the canton having authority to summon the other cantons to meet together. Between some of the cantons there was a slighter bond than between others. Zurich, Schwyz, Uri, Unterwalden, and Luzern, formed no foreign alliance without mutual consent. Glarus, Zug, and Berne, each did in this respect as it pleased, but all these eight were bound to support each other's form of government. The other five cantons, Fribourg, Soleure, Basle, Schaffhausen, and Appenzell, were much more independent, both of the rest and of each other, and chose their own allies both at home and abroad. We need only add, that the Swiss army was a militia, consisting of all the males from sixteen to sixty, one-third being enrolled in regiments. Thus a body of nine thousand six hundred were available for the defense of the whole country in case of sudden invasion, to be assembled and directed on such an emergency by deputies from all the states nominated for the purpose.

Such was the political constitution of the Helvetic republics, of which a comparatively quiet development forms their history during the last century; and certainly a group of governments so diversified, individually and specifically, and yet so plainly of one generic description, has been found nowhere else so situated and conjoined in ancient or modern times.

CHAPTER VII.

OVERTHROW AND RESTORATION.

The French revolution was the revolution of all Europe. Every kingdom and state was more or less affected by that tremendous concussion of principles and parties. The sentiments of the revolutionists awakened sympathy among the oppressed or dissatisfied everywhere, and the attempts of the old monarchy to stem the swelling torrent excited a friendly interest on the part of other governments. The military spirit and projects of the republic soon involved the continent in war, and powers which originally had no wish to take any part in it were forced into the fearful strife. From the commencement of those movements in France which led to the subversion of the throne, different parties in that country found favour with corresponding parties among the Swiss. But the policy of the confederated cantons was neutral. Interference on the part of the government in the struggles of the neighboring kingdom was studiously avoided ; yet events after a time brought the united republics of Helvetia within the whirl of the tremendous maelstrom, in whose waters their independence was ingulfed, till at the general peace it was restored and secured. The massacre of the Swiss guards in Paris on the 10th of August, 1792, does not properly belong to the history of Switzerland; for those ill-fated men were only individual mercenaries in the monarch's pay. Their horrible death, however, threw many a Swiss family into mourning, and must have produced deep feelings, as regarded the revolution, in a thousand breasts. The first great overt act which connected Switzerland with the French revolution, was the occupation of Basle by a French army, and its annexation to the new republic in 1793. Geneva, with its old French relations, was not likely to remain in safety and quietude; revolutionary agents were at work there, fanning the embers of civil strife, which for so many years had been occasionally bursting out. A reign of terror occurred in the city in 1794. The atrocities of Paris were repeated, only on a less scale. Forty were formally condemned to death, and a hundred were exiled; but a large number besides were shot by an infuriated mob, while many more suffered from fines and imprisonment. Order was restored, and the little Genevese republic returned to its old constitution in the course of a year, but in other parts of Switzerland there were disturbances. The rural populations of Zurich and St. Gall sought to gain redress of their grievances, but with very different results: the former failing in their attempt, and suffering heavy punishment for their agitation; the latter securing some considerable advantages from their abbot lord, which made him very popular among his dependents.

For some time the French Directory professed to respect the neutrality of the Swiss. A public audience was given in the Luxembourg to the minister of the confederation, and its flag was hung up in the convention hall, beside that of the United States. Diplomatic notes, however, were constantly sent to the governments of the cantons, full of complaints about their giving asylum to French emigrants, and demanding their immediate expulsion. These, with other charges and requirements, irritated the Swiss authorities; yet, fearful of further provoking their powerful neighbors, they manifested the most remarkable moderation and patience. The unfriendliness of France toward Switzerland increased after the triumph of the new Directory. Anxious to possess the Alps, as an outpost against Austria, and fixing its eyes on the city coffers of Berne, Zurich, and Basle, the unprincipled government of the revolution had no difficulty in creating a ground of quarrel. The Pays de Vaud was subject to Berne; the former complained of the latter, and aimed at the revival of certain political rights which, whether in form extinguished or not, had long been waived. The people of the country, wearied of the yoke of their city masters, proceeded to open revolt; a petition was got up among them and forwarded to the French Directory, which at once espoused their cause. Under the hypocritical pretense of giving freedom to the oppressed, and of putting down tyrannical aristocracies, one body of French troops speedily appeared on the frontiers of the Pays de Vaud, and another on the northern borders of Berne. It was demanded of the Bernese that they should expel the English minister. This, they said, was impossible; but for their sakes he withdrew. It was then required that they should expel all emigrants. This was evaded by a counter-demand on the part of the Swiss. Then it was asked that all decorations received by Swiss officers from the French monarchy should be laid aside. This was granted. But still there was no peace for Switzerland: Bonaparte's army seized on the Grison country, after which, as the general returned to France by way of Berne and Basle, he treated the authorities of the former with contempt, but expressed much favor toward the latter city, which was already a part of the revolutionary republic, while the most violent sentiments were rife among the peasantry of the canton. A club of the "friends of liberty," as they called themselves, was shortly afterward formed under French influence, and the result was the dissolution of the old cantonal government, and the temporary deposit of power in the hands of sixty persons chosen from all classes. The Helvetic confederacy was now evidently on the brink of ruin; a diet was held at Aargau, to consult respecting the general welfare; an attempt was made to imitate the memorable scene at Rutli, by the deputies swearing to maintain the liberties of their common country; but it was a mere farce; they talked, but did nothing. Basle had withdrawn from them; and as soon as the diet broke up, there was an insurrection at the place of meeting. Aargau was subject to Berne. The dependency now threw off its allegiance, and planted in the streets the tree of liberty: the revolt spread. Berne, threatened by a French army, thus found itself also involved in a domestic revolution. The disaffected were encouraged by the success of the Pays de Vaud, which had shaken off the yoke of Berne—thanks to the arms of France. Power thus crumbling into pieces on all sides, the government of the canton met full of consternation; plans of reform were proposed; concessions were made to the democratic spirit now dayly gaining ground. Other cantons, moved by fear, adopted a similar course. But neither in Berne nor elsewhere had the authorities a full comprehension of their own danger. It was thought the approaching evils might be staved off, and a sort of superstitious confidence existed in reference to the stability of the confederation, which had weathered so many storms. The Bernese senators therefore temporized and vacillated; they were not the men for the crisis, though it is much easier for us to administer blame now than it was for them to act in a manner becoming their position then. While in Switzerland there were wanting both wisdom and courage, the French, as sagacious and bold as they were unprincipled, pushed on their plans, and took possession of Mulhausen and Geneva. They forced those cities to join the French republic, and then represented them as seeking "the honor," and as surrendering the old constitution to obtain it.

To add to the confusion and misery of the period, the Bernese soldiers were exasperated by the irresolution of the government. D'Erlach, their brave and patriotic general, received orders and counter-orders, which showed that the executive had lost its strength and also its reason. The Swiss forces were disposed in bad positions, contingents did not come in time, whole troops deserted, while the French triumphantly marched on toward Berne. There were thirty thousand Frenchmen; the army opposed to them did not consist of more than half that number: all was in confusion. The council of Berne, in a moment of agony, dissolved and proclaimed a provisional regency; a conciliatory message was sent to the French, which was haughtily received, and served not at all to stay their progress. Mutiny had begun among the Swiss army owing to the conduct of the rulers, and some of the officers were slain. On the 5th of March, 1797, an engagement took place at Laupen, and the French were repulsed; on the same day a fatal reverse was experienced by D'Erlach, under whom the Bernese were defeated at Frauenbrunnen, in the immediate neighborhood of their own city; two thousand Swiss were killed and wounded, and the loss of the French amounted to three-fourths of that number. Berne immediately surrendered, and the terrible tragedy ended in the further mutiny of the soldiers, who, deeming themselves betrayed, actually murdered their officers in cold blood! Among the victims was D'Erlach himself; and it afterward appeared that the assassins had been stimulated to this villanous and cruel act by forged documents which they had received from the French, as proofs of their general's treachery! "More than one hundred officers, including twelve members of the great council, and most of them belonging to the principal families of Berne, were killed on that fatal day; their names are registered in golden letters upon six marble slabs placed in one of the aisles of the Cathedral of Berne. Such was the fall of Berne, a republic that had existed for nearly six hundred years. It fell by the same acts, the same hands, and nearly about the same time as Venice and Genoa; like them it exhibited weakness and hesitation in its councils; but, unlike them, it showed something of old Swiss determination in the hour of its struggle, and it fell neither unhonored nor unmourned."—*Vieusseux.*

The occupation of Zurich, and the whole north of Switzerland by the French army, immediately succeeded, while the treasures of Berne were carried off to Paris, and further levies were made in Switzerland upon the impudent ground that the country ought to pay for its liberation. All the proceedings of the Directory in reference to Switzerland, it is said, were carried on without ever consulting the legislative council of the French republic; and even an ex-director, Carnot, afterward acknowledged that it was an impious war, realizing to the letter the well-known fable of the wolf and the lamb. A new constitution was soon prepared for Switzerland by its masters, and the cantons were summoned to send deputies to Aargau for its adoption; but the mountaineers of the Waldstatter refused, and backed their refusal by taking up arms under Aloys Reding. Terrible was the resistance of these men, in whom the spirit of their fathers burned anew, and terrible was the revenge they wreaked on the French soldiery, whose atrocious excesses had roused their intense indignation. Aloys Reding was able to extort honorable terms from his enemies; but a different termination came to another struggle by the people of Unterwalden, whose country was ravaged in the most awful manner with fire and sword. In the church-yard of the little town of Stanz a chapel stands, erected to the memory of four hundred and fourteen people, including one hundred and two women and twenty-five children, all of whom were murdered together by the French on the 9th September, 1797. The heroism of Reding is also commemorated on a stone which bears his name near the outlet of the lake of Thun, on which Wordsworth composed the following lines:—

"Around a wild and woody hill,
  A gravel pathway heading,
We reach a votive stone, that bears
  The name of Aloys Reding.

"Well judged the friend who placed it there,
  For silence and protection,
And happily with a finer care
  Of dutiful affection,

"The sun regards it from the west,
  And while in summer glory
He sets, his sinking yields a type
  Of that pathetic story.

"And oft he tempts the patriot Swiss
  Around the grove to linger;
Till all is dim, save this bright stone,
  Touch'd by his golden finger."

The occupation of Switzerland by the French continued till 1801. It was a period of the deepest distress to the inhabitants. All kinds of misery which could be inflicted by a brutal soldiery were endured. To add to the sorrows of this unhappy country, it was invaded by Austrians and Russians, after the outbreak of a fresh war between the Emperor of Germany and the French republic. Zurich and St. Gothard were scenes of dreadful engagements, especially the latter, on whose mountain passes the army of the allies met their enemies, and fought with ferocious energy, hurling one another down the rocks, and dyeing the stream of the Ruess with the blood of the slain. The peasantry suffered from both parties, who unceremoniously seized upon their humble possessions; spoiling them of their flocks, occupying their homesteads, and appropiating their harvests. One-fourth of the Schwyz canton was reduced to beggary. Between six and seven hundred persons in one valley were left utterly destitute. Among the Grisons, where the inhabitants rose up to defend themselves against the troublers of their peace, the French took unmerciful revenge; women were hunted like beasts, and shot with infants in their arms in the half-frozen Lake of Toma.

After the peace of Luneville in 1801, the French evacuated Switzerland. The new constitution was found utterly abortive, and the civil affairs of the country were thrown into complete disorder. French agents were the only *real* governors, and they treated Switzerland as a conquered country, seizing upon public and private property as need or avarice might prompt. To the credit of such of the Swiss as the French Directory intrusted with the carrying out of the new constitution, it ought to be stated that they never imitated their masters in the way of confiscation and punishment. They did not erect a revolutionary tribunal; they enforced no proscriptions; they reared no scaffolds; they filled no dungeons. The useless puppet-show of the Helvetic Directory, as the Swiss executive was called, was soon put down by its creators, and a new constitution was devised. There was to be one Helvetic republic, and Berne was to be the capital; but this project, though adopted at a diet, came to nothing. A third constitution was afterward framed; but the forest cantons, opposed to centralization, upon which these schemes were based, endeavored to revive their old confederacy. Different factions now arose. The flame of discord began to blaze; Switzerland was on the brink of a civil war; when, in 1803, Napoleon, who, though unfriendly to the old aristocratic governments of the Helvetic confederacy, had never desired the entire overthrow of Swiss independence, interfered, and summoned to Paris the representatives of different parties and interests, on whom he urged the reorganization of affairs in the several cantons according to their peculiar character, including the restoration of the pure democracies, and the reform and liberalization of the aristocratic governments. He impressed upon them the impossibility of reducing their country under one republic, and urged "that a federal diet, consisting of deputies named by the various cantons, should assemble every year in one of the principal towns, and decide upon all matters which concern the whole confederation, as well as mediate in all differences between one canton and another; and that there should be no central directing canton, but that the landamman of the canton where the diet meets for the year should transact all federal affairs." This was the famous *act of mediation* which restored peace to Switzerland. In harmony with Napoleon's directions, a constitution was framed and adopted; and though the peasantry in some parts at first refused to submit to it, obedience was at length enforced, and order and tranquillity ensued.

Napoleon's mediation in the affairs of Switzerland was, perhaps, the most liberal act in his whole political life; it was certainly the one in which he observed the conditions most faithfully.

During the eleven momentous years which followed throughout the headlong career of his ambition, in the midst of the gigantic wars of the empire, he respected his own work, the independence of Switzerland. That little country, surrounded by immense armies, rested in peace amid the din of battle and the crash of falling empires. No foreign soldier stepped over its tranquil boundaries, and it was the only remaining asylum on the continent where individual security and freedom were still to be found. The Swiss were the only people exempt from the tyrannical code of the conscription; they furnished, however, a body of sixteen thousand men to the French service, as they had done under the old monarchy, but it was raised and kept effective by means of voluntary enlistment. He, however, took care to enforce his continental system on Switzerland, and would not allow them to import English goods. Manufactures and commerce revived; agriculture was improved; a great deal of land was drained; and encouragement was given to literature, science, and education.

The act of mediation was dissolved in 1814, when the tutelage of the French emperor over Switzerland came to an end. The cantons assembled to reconsider their constitution. The basis was laid for a new federal union of nineteen independent cantons.* To these the Valais, Neuchâtel, and Geneva, were afterward added, making the number twenty-two. The Congress of Vienna in 1815 acknowledged the independence and neutrality of the Swiss, and on the 7th of August the new compact was solemnly adopted at Zurich. "This federal fact," says Franscini, "whether of good or imperfection, has been the work of the Swiss themselves. It contains principles entirely national; some of which date from the oldest times of Swiss independence, while others are taken from the act of mediation of 1803, or are improvements upon the latter." The independency of each canton as to its internal affairs was hereby guaranteed, provision was made for the raising of troops in the proportion of one to fifty of the population, and a war fund created by the enactment of levies on foreign imports. The diet was formed to consist of deputies from the twenty-two cantons, each canton having but one vote. An executive was appointed for the administration of federal affairs during the suspension of sittings. War, peace, and alliances were left to be determined by the diet, on all

* Zurich, Berne, Luzern, Uri, Schwyz, Unterwalden, Glarus, Zug, Fribourg, Solothurn, Basle, Schaff hausen, Appenzell, St. Gall, the Grisons, Aargau, Thurgau, Ticino, Vaud.

which questions a majority of three-fourths was rendered requisite. To it was confided the appointment of diplomatic agents, and the making provision for the general safety of the country; while it was also authorized to appoint an arbitrator and umpires for the settlement of disputes between one canton and another.

Such is a very general description of the principles of the Swiss confederacy as determined upon in 1815, and as they are still on the whole maintained among these interesting republics. Changes took place in the internal constitution of the aristocratic cantons. The country, as well as the town, was admitted to return members to the legislature in the proportion of one-third, and monopolies—another old source of discord—were abolished. The democratic cantons remained much the same as before, and the new ones, Aargau, Thurgau, Vaud, Ticino, and St. Gall, were framed on the basis of an equality of rights; while Neuchâtel, it should be stated, was restored as an appendage to the Prussian crown.

Switzerland remained at peace from 1815 to 1830. "The general condition of the country might be called prosperous. Civil and criminal laws in most cantons remained as they had been of old, defective and encumbered with the rust of the middle ages. The education was improved in several districts, but not all over the country, no general system of popular instruction being enforced. The press was, in most of the cantons, under a strict censorship. The sittings of the cantonal councils and of the federal diet were kept close, and no report of their discussions was published. In short, most of the Swiss states, although under republican names and forms, were really less popular in their institutions than several of the constitutional monarchies of Europe. The same men remained in power and office as if they had been appointed for life." Dissatisfaction was the result. Disturbances arose in 1830. They spread through the country, and Switzerland witnessed another general revolution. The tangled threads of its history we cannot here unravel; but the state into which the governments afterward settled down will be briefly noticed in a subsequent part of this volume.

PART II.—DESCRIPTIVE.

Having completed our very brief sketch of Swiss history, we propose to notice the interesting country itself which has been the theater of so many stirring events, and the stage on which has been developed so remarkable a system of republican institutions.

It is a small territory, about two hundred and ten miles in length from east to west, and about one hundred and thirty in breadth from north to south. Adjoining the plains of Lombardy on the Italian side, the plains of Burgundy on the French side, and the plains of Swabia on the German side, it lifts itself above the level of the European continent, and throws up those lofty mountains which are its defense, its ornaments, and its glory. Even the lower parts of the country are one thousand two hundred feet above the level of the sea, and one thousand feet higher than the level of northern Italy. Its surface is distributed into mountain and table-land, the former yielding those beautiful and magnificent prospects which the traveler goes from far to see; while the latter is also full of pictorial and picturesque interest, and presents characteristic features and claims in its rich fertility and its thriving towns, its natural productions, and its forms of human industry. The plateau of Switzerland forms one-half of the whole country, occupying its whole breadth from south-west to north-east, and including the cantons of Vaud and Fribourg, the larger part of Berne, almost the whole of Luzern and Aargau, Zurich, Zug, and Thurgau entirely, and a considerable part of St. Gall. The mountain region will be described as we proceed; but before we enter on any notices of its character and scenery, it may be proper briefly to observe that Switzerland has its iron mines in the Jura, coal in Fribourg, Basle, and Thurgau, rich veins of lead and zinc in the country of the Grisons, rock salt in the canton of Vaud, and salt springs abundantly in various places; that it has mineral waters in the Valais, and Aargau and Berne and Vaud and St. Gall; that its lakes are full of fish, especially trout, and that its rivers abound in tench and and carp perch and salmon; that the hare and the partridge find cover amid the maple, the birch, the beech, and the oak, which clothe the sides of the mountains; that bears and wolves invest the higher regions, where also the fleet chamois leaps from crag to crag, and leads the chase of the sportsman; while birds of prey, the vulture and the eagle, build among the rocks, and sail over the glaciers, and whirl round the snowy peaks.

In the arrangement of this second portion of our little volume, we propose to notice Switzerland as it is, under the three-fold aspect of *nature*, *art*, and *society*, not altogether overlooking such associations as may present themselves to our mind in connection with them.

CHAPTER I.

NATURE.

WE shall begin by calling attention to the mountains of Switzerland.

The Jura range, sloping on the French side and abrupt on the Swiss, divides the two countries by its slightly curved line, running in a north-easterly direction, for about one hundred and fifty miles, from the banks of the Rhone, near Mount Vauche in Savoy, to the banks of the Aar near Soleure, and onward toward the Rhine near Basle. It is not a single ridge, but a number of mountain masses, sometimes lying parallel and sometimes branching out in spurs; the whole presenting a variety of scene, consisting of rounded summits, broad table-lands, and deep valleys. Its highest point is not more than five thousand five hundred feet above the level of the sea.

Among the many passes of the Jura, we may mention three of the great gateways to Switzerland, much frequented by travelers, from the west and north. The first is by Mijoux and Gex; but as they are in France, we shall not notice the scenery there. The other passes, of which we have a delightful recollection, are the Upper and Lower Hauenstein; the former on the high road from Basle to Soleure, the latter on the high road from Basle to Luzern. We have entered Switzerland by the latter, and how beautiful is the road all the way from the old city, by the banks of the Rhone, to the foot of the pass at Bakten, —calmly, sweetly beautiful. There begins the ascent amid scenery very grand, and rather rich than wild; and as one proceeds, the overflowing fullness of the verdure, the deep green of the valleys, the strips of corn which variegate them like gold veins in an emerald basin, delight the eye and quicken the imagination. At the top of the pass, the view, looking down on the broad deep valley to the south-east, which there opens, is charming in the extreme; and as the road advances, distant views of the Alps appear, and the snowy tops are seen, whiter than alabaster, lifting themselves up against the clear blue sky like clouds full of light ascending from the horizon. We have twice left Switzerland by the Upper Hauenstein. It is soon reached after leaving Soleure. The mountains are much grander, more rugged, stern, and sublime, than about the former pass. They assume a castellated form, and the valley between of brilliant hue looks like the smoothly shaven lawn of some baronial hall. Woods hang like green drapery down the walls of rock, and the fortress of Talkenstein juts over the road, as if it were some eagle's nest; while houses and orchards dot and enliven the towns and sides of the vale. Issuing from the gorge, the traveler sees before him another mountain range, another branch of the Jura, resembling a second rampart, inclosing a second castle court. Then the pass becomes narrower as the road ascends, and winds round the outstretched limbs of these immense hills. Some views further on reminded us of the finest part of the north of Devon, only the cottages sprinkled over the rocks gave the place that unmistakeable Swiss character which the eye at once recognizes. Here and there a castle on the heights imparts additional interest and character to the scene.

The Weissenstein, at the back of Soleure, is one

of those summits in Switzerland, from which, as a lofty observatory, the most commanding panoramic views are obtained. The Alps here are seen in the extreme distance, the chain extending its links of snow for a length of two hundred miles, from Sentis to Mont Blanc. This is the southern line of the picture. To the south-east are the Bernese Alps, showing the Jungfrau, Schreckhorn, and other peaks; while the space between all those sublime regions and the point of sight is filled up by wooded vales, the Lakes of Morat, Neuchâtel, and Bienne, and the winding of the river Aar. Another celebrated view from the Jura mountains is on the summit of Claremont, just above Neuchâtel. On a very clear day the view is even more magnificent in the judgment of some than that from the Weissenstein.

The Alps form by far the grander portion of the mountains of Switzerland. They enter the country on the south-west from Savoy, bearing the name of the Pennine ranges, and dividing Switzerland from Italy. Some very high peaks are in this region, Mount Velan belonging to the St. Bernard group eleven thousand feet high, the Matterhorn fourteen thousand eight hundred, and Mount Rosa fifteen thousand one hundred and fifty. Then comes the great St. Gothard mass, which forms a center, whence branches shoot out in various directions; the Bernese, the Alps of Glarus, the Rhætian Alps, and another mountain band reaching down to the Pennine. Among these are summits from nine thousand to twelve thousand feet. Another vast assemblage of Alps is situated to the north-east of St. Gothard, covering the Grison country, and furrowed by not less than sixty deep valleys. Generally, with regard to these "everlasting hills," it may be remarked that their majestic elevation may be divided into distinct bands, or regions, marked by characteristic vegetation, till they reach the point where all vegetation ceases. The lowest step, which gently slopes and is covered with a rich soil, is industriously cultivated, and abundantly repays the toils of the husbandman. Then comes the wood region, covered with huge forests of firs and other trees. Above that is the Alp proper, or pasture region, the place for hardy wild flowers and grass. Moss and lichens border the crest of rocks where vegetation stops; sometimes the summits are covered with meadow-land, and herds and flocks graze on the very top. When the mountain rises above the snow line, you have noble white cones, and pinnacles, and domes, such as Rosa, the Jungfrau, and Mont Blanc.

The passes among the Alps are incomparably more grand than those of the Jura. Beauty predominant in the one is exchanged for the predominance of sublimity in the other—sublimity in many cases very terrible. Of the fifty and more Alpine passes we can only speak here of a very few. To take the following, which are well known, the traveler will probably range them in his recollections in some such order as this:—First, the Brunig, from Lungern to Meyringen, as the easiest and gentlest, with its woods and little slips of arable and pasture land, and the grand view of the vale of Meyringen at the south end of the pass. Next comes the Scheideck, by which the traveler from the south approaches the wonders of the Oberland, passing by the beautiful Rosenlau, with its rich wild flowers, and then threading forests of fir, through which the Jungfrau and other peaks shine down upon the path like galaxies of jewels, till the magnificent descent to Grindelwald brings in sight the whole of that vale with its glaciers and ravines. The Grimsel with the Falls of the Aar, and the Furca with the glacier of the Rhone, both lying between Meyringen and St. Gothard, will probably then occur to the memory, with all their wild, bare, rugged, and desolate associations, and thoughts of a weary march on the edge of precipices and over fragments of rock, and through marshy swamps. The Gemmi, leading from Kandersteg to Leuch, will contest the palm of the stern and terrible with the Grimsel and the Furca, while its rocks scattered in confusion as if an earthquake had upheaved the hills—and the long snow-drifts in summer—and the dead-looking tarn or lake by the wayside—and the dreary walk for miles and miles, without seeing a house, or a creature, or a tree—and the precipitous descent at last to Leuch, down the winding stair of the rock, will come to mind; making the contrast of the warm home fireside on a winter's evening very, very pleasant, as the pictorial panorama of the whole scene glides before the imagination. The three great passes over the Alps to Italy will crown these recollections. The first is the Simplon, commencing on the Swiss side at the little town of Brieg, and terminating at Domo d'Ossola on the Italian side. Winding in a zigzag direction, carried over chasms, and penetrating through rocks, with all the general objects of Alpine scenery, such as steep precipices, overhanging pines, dizzy-looking bridges, and thundering cataracts, the road commands on the Swiss side near Pearsal an amazingly grand view of the Bernese Alps with their glittering points; and on the Italian side presents now one of those gorges with precipitous sides which arrest the traveler's steps, and furnish such abundant material for the artist's pencil; and then a charming map of Italian beauty, full of maize fields, and vineyards, and villages, with tall white campanilles, under a sky of the clearest and richest azure. The second is the St. Gothard, beginning at Amsteg and ending at Bellinzona. Running to Andermatt on rocky ledges by the side of the roaring Reuss, and crossing it by the Devil's Bridge, where there is one of the largest and wildest of Swiss waterfalls; then winding in a zigzag shape, like all other pathways over these regions, the road scales the summit, a bare, bleak, windy spot, six thousand eight hundred and eight feet above the level of the sea, and then descends toward Airolo, looking down into the romantic valleys of the Ticino, passing by picturesque rocks, especially the Dazio Grande, a rent in Monte Piottino, sweeping along the Val Levantina, and revealing as it approaches Italy all the exquisite features which pertain to the scenery of that land. The third is the Splügen, on the way to which from Zurich the traveler is to blame if he do not stop to see the baths of Pfeffers, in a narrow ravine where the light of day is almost excluded, and a wild mountain stream boils along at the bottom. The Via Mala, the most interesting part of the Splügen, is not entered till you have passed Thusis. There begins some of the most gloomy and sublime scenery in all Switzerland, formed by rocks beetling overhead, while the Rhine rolls in the deep bottom of the ravine. Wonderful views are obtained from the bridges which cross the gulf, the rocks beneath in some instances meeting so as to overlap one another and to conceal the foaming waters. The middle bridge, as it is called, is four hundred feet above the stream, yet in the fearful inundation of 1834 it rose to within a few feet of the spring of the arch. The road is a shelf cut along the side of a rock, and what the traveler sees and hears is sure to fill him with emotions which it were useless to endeavor to describe in words. The village of Splügen is situated further on, beyond which is the summit of the pass, six thousand eight hundred and fourteen feet high, near the Austrian boundary. The descent to Italy opens a succession of noble views, and after crossing the magnificent waterfall of the Medessino, the road reaches Campo Dolcino, an ugly place with a beautiful name; beyond which huge fragments of rocks, grown over by majestic chestnuts, form a succession of objects exquisitely pictorial, the green foliage and the brown rock, with the white campanille, forming a delightful harmony of colors.

Among the many Alpine objects of leading interest are the sides and crowns of the snow mountains, shining with a dazzling whiteness in the summer's sun. Those who have seen the Jungfrau from the Wengern Alps will ever afterward dwell on it as among the richest of memory's pictures. So clear and unencumbered, it stands out with a mantle of snow hanging down its gigantic shoulders, and presenting such a field of brilliant whiteness that the eye is compelled to turn for relief to the green slopes on the opposite side. It is the region of avalanches. Every day in summer they may be heard breaking with the noise of thunder, and appearing, when they meet the traveler's eye, like a stream of snow, winding down a mountain side, till, at the bottom, it curls into folds, like the convolutions of a silver snake. But these summer avalanches, it may be here remarked, are very different from those of which we so often read, as having inflicted fearful injuries on the dwellers of the mountain regions. The harmless avalanches, on which the tourist looks which so much interest, are called glacier, or ice avalanches. Others are divided into three classes, and are phenomena of a terrific character. The *drift* avalanches are composed of loose snow, when it is dislodged from its position for want of support, which is often the case in the winter months, and is attributable, according to the opinion of scientific men, to the impulse of the wind. The *sliding* avalanches are formed by huge masses of frozen snow, and originate in the middle region of the mountains, when the natural warmth of the earth has melted the icy bonds, and left a slippery descent. The *creeping* avalanches are similar, but are confined to gentler declivities, and derive their distinction from the comparative slowness of their motion. The first of these are the most destructive; the second are not without injury; the last are generally harmless.

From the top of the Col de Balme, looking into the Valley of Chamouni, a magnificent sight is obtained of Mont Blanc. From this point the monarch of mountains, when seen as it was by ourselves for a few minutes completely unclouded, appears grand and impressive in the extreme. There he was, as if seated on a throne, with his guards around him, and the glaciers penetrating into the valley seeming like the ermine borders of his robes. The Flégère is another eminence, much resorted to as an observatory from which to gaze on the hoary father of the Alps. The Brevin, loftier, and of more fatiguing ascent, is a still more favorable point from which to gain the coveted sight of the mount in his majesty. Until lately, the summit of the Jungfrau had not been scaled. The feat was accomplished by some peasants in 1828; and afterward, in 1841, by Professor Forbes, and some scientific friends. The ascent of Mont Blanc, though loftier than the Jungfrau, (the former being fifteen thousand five hundred and twenty-six, the latter only thirteen thousand seven hundred and eighteen feet,) has been several times accomplished, and the adventures connected with it have now become familiar to a multitude of persons by graphic and pictorial representations.

Another ascent of a different kind, and for a different purpose, is made by hundreds of tourists every summer to the top of the Righi, near Luzern. The pathway from Arth winds through a very romantic region, and behind the traveler there lie the scattered fragments of the huge land slip of the Rossberg, the fall of which caused such tremendous devastation in the valley, sweeping away cottages, cattle, and human beings. Toiling up, from station to station, the pedestrian gladly stops ever and anon to look on the glorious views he is leaving; and when he has attained the summit, what a panorama breaks on him of lands and lakes—of heroic memories associated with the name of Tell and Winkelried; for on one side is the lake of the four cantons, on the other the field of Sempach. But the greatest sight of all is the clear sunrise tinging the mountain tops. Having been disappointed of this spectacle ourselves, we must here trust to the pen of others. And as the phenomenon is so exceedingly beautiful and grand, we shall venture on inserting two accounts of it from different pens, the first from that of Dr. Forbes :—

"We were roused shortly after four by the loud notes of an Alpine horn, blown in the gallery of the house; and all the party were soon assembled on the highest point of the Rigi-Kulm. The morning was bright and without a cloud, showing all the views much more distinctly than on the preceding evening. The air was, however, very cold to our feelings, and we required all our coats to keep us warm while awaiting the sunrise. The thermometer showed the same temperature as last night, 52°. The sunrise was glorious, and the clearness of the atmosphere enabled us to observe distinctly the beautiful phenomenon, so often seen afterward, of the gradual illumination of the snowy peaks, according to their height and the progressive descent of the line of light on them as the sun ascended. After satiating and almost tiring our eyes by long and manifold speculations of the grand scenes on all sides of us, near and remote, we returned to the hotel, and having completed our toilet, partook of a very fair breakfast of coffee, etc., and then started on our return to Goldau about half-past six."

So much for Dr. Forbes's description. The following is from the pen of Dr. Cheever, and glows with a poetic fervor more worthy of the theme:—

"It was the 6th of September, and the most perfectly beautiful morning that can be imagined. At a quarter past three the stars were reigning supreme in the heavens, with just enough of the old moon left to make a trail of light in the shape of a little silver boat among them. But speedily the horizon began to redden over the eastern fringe of mountains, and then the dawn stole on in such a succession of deepening tints, that nothing but the hues of the preceding sunset could be more beautiful. But there is this great difference between the sunrise and the sunset, that the hues of sunset are every moment deepening as you look upon them until again they fade into the darkness, while those of the sunrise gradually fade into the light of day. It is difficult to say which process is most beautiful; for if you could make everything stand still around you, if you could stereotype or stay the process for an hour, you could not tell whether it were the morning dawn or evening twilight. A few long thin stripes of fleecy cloud lay motionless above the eastern horizon, like layers of silver lace, dipped first in crimson, then in gold, then in pink, then lined with an ermine of light, just as if the moon had been lengthened in soft furrows along the sky. This scene in the east attracts every eye at first, but it is not here that the glory of the view is to be looked for. This glory is in that part of the horizon on which the sun first falls as he struggles up behind the mountains to flood the world with light. And the reason why it is so glorious is because, long before you call it sunrise in the east, he lights up in the west a range of colossal pyres, that look like blazing cressets kindled from the sky and fed with naphtha. The object most conspicuous as the dawn broke, and indeed the most sublimely beautiful, was the vast enormous range of the snowy mountains of the Oberland, without spot or vail of cloud or mist to dim them; the Finster Aarhorn at the left, and the Jungfrau and Silberhorn at the right, peak after peak and mass after mass, glittering with a cold wintry whiteness in the gray dawn. Almost the exact half of the circumference of the horizon, commanded before and behind in our view, was filled with these peaks and masses of snow and ice; then, lower down, the mountains of bare rock, and lower still the earth with mounds of verdure. And this section of the horizontal circumference, which is filled with the vast ranges of the Oberland Alps, being almost due west from the sun's first appearance, it is on their tops that the rising rays first strike.

"This was the scene for which we watched, and it seems as if nothing in nature can ever again be so beautiful. It was as if an angel had flown round the horizon of mountain ranges, and lighted up each of their white pyramidal points in succession, like a row of gigantic lamps burning with rosy fires. Just so the sun suddenly tipped the highest points and lines of the snowy outline; and then, descending lower on the body of the mountains, it was as if an invisible omnipotent Hand had taken them and dipped the whole range in a glowing pink; the hue between the cold snow untouched by the sunlight, and the warm roseate hue above, remaining perfectly distinct. This effect continued some minutes, becoming, up to a certain point, more and more beautiful.

"We were like children in a dark room, watching for the lighting up of some great transparency; or, to use that image with which the poet Dante endeavored to describe the expectant gaze of Beatrice in Paradise, awaiting the splendors to be revealed, we might say, connecting some passages and adapting the imagery—

'E'en as the bird who, 'midst the leafy bower,
Has in her nest sat darkling through the night
With her sweet brood; impatient to descry
Their wished looks, and to bring home their food,
In the fond quest unconscious of her toil:
She of the time prevenient, on the spray
That overhangs their couch, with wakeful gaze
Expects the sun; nor ever till the dawn
Removeth from the east her eager ken.
Wistfully thus we look'd to see the heavens
Wax more and more resplendent, till on earth
Her mountain peaks burn'd as with rosy flame.
'Twixt gladness and amaze,
In sooth no will had we to utter aught
Or hear. And as a pilgrim, when he rests
Within the temple of his vow, looks round,
In breathless awe, and hopes some time to tell
Of all its goodly state; e'en so our eyes
Coursed up and down along the living light,
Now low, and now aloft, and now around,
Visiting every step. Each mount did seem
Colossal ruby whereon so inwrought
The sunbeam glow'd, yet soft, it flamed intense
In ecstasy of glory.'

"In truth, no word was uttered when that scene became visible. Each gazed in silence, or spake as in a whisper. It was as if we witnessed some supernatural revelation, where mighty spirits were the actors between earth and heaven—

'With such ravishing light
And mantling crimson, in transparent air,
The splendors shot before us.'

"And yet a devout soul might have almost felt, seeing those fires kindled as on the altars of God made visible, as if it heard the voices of seraphim crying, 'Holy, holy, holy, is the Lord of hosts: the whole earth is full of his glory!' For indeed the vision was so radiant, so full of sudden and unimaginable beauty and splendor, that methinks a phalanx of the sons of God, who might have been passing at that moment, could not have helped stopping and shouting for joy as on the morning of creation."

To return to more general descriptions. The mountains, as seen from the valleys, are very sublime. As the ridges wind and branch out and intersect, of course, as beheld from the bottom, a number of the peaks are hidden, and it is difficult to estimate the height of those which are visible; but to look at them from that point of view, is to enjoy a variety of vision which, combined with the remembrance of the sight from lofty points, adds greatly to the enjoyment of the spectator. The beauty of many of the valleys enhances the value of the whole picture; the verdure of the fields, the foliage of the orchard and wood, and the silver waters of the cascade, standing out in relief upon the background of rock and glacier and snow mountain. For example, the view of the Jungfrau, from the charming vale of Lauterbrunnen, so worthy of its name, (nothing but fountains,) and views of other peaks from the opposite vale of Grindelwald, and views again of the same from the vale of Rosenlau, and views of the mountains on the side of the broad valley of the Rhone, and especially views of Mont Blanc and the neighboring summits from the rich vale of Chamouni; these imprint themselves on the mind with a charm which no lover of nature can soon "let die." To see them as the morning breaks, rich in roseate hues, and after the sun has risen on them, long before the valley has caught his rays, burning in purest light—and at mid-day looking so cool on the traveler amid sultry heat—and at eventide again throwing back the slanting beams in varied colors—and after sunset, amid the pale radiance of the moon, standing like angel watchmen round the region, with stars glimmering overhead—all this awakens the deepest enthusiasm of the soul, and satisfies the love of the beautiful, and suggests manifold similitudes of still purer and holier things, and raises the thoughts to that Infinite One who made them all, and sustains them all, and who gives to man what enables him to enjoy them all.

From this general account of Swiss mountains, we proceed to a notice of the Swiss *glaciers.*

There are few things of which it is more difficult to convey a correct idea to those who have not seen them. They are often confounded with snow mountains, but though connected with them, they are distinct phenomena, being composed of that part of the snow which is converted into ice. They lie below the snow line in deep hollows, as if they were frozen lakes, or droop over the side of a valley as if they were frozen cataracts. Most numerous are they in Switzerland, being not less than six hundred in number, covering altogether a surface of fifty German square miles; connected with Mont Blanc there are seventeen or eighteen. When the fact of their being ice and not snow is fully realized, still persons are apt to misimagine their appearance; for they are by no means smooth, like our frozen lakes and rivers, but present a very unequal surface, undulating, furrowed, and broken. Nor is the ice itself like ours when thoroughly frozen, but rather resembles it when the process of freezing has just commenced, and sharp crystals are formed on the face of the water. After all these qualifications are apprehended and received, poetical fancy will be apt to paint the glacier as an expanse all white and pure, the crystals glittering in the sunbeams—the field of ice looking like a sea of glass. The traveler who comes upon the Grindelwald glacier, whether upper or lower, having never beheld one before, feels much disappointment at so pleasing an illusion being dispelled, for dispelled it is most completely. The glaciers bend over into the valley, and present at a distance the aspect of huge heaps of very dirty snow, with a strong tinge of blue in some parts; it reminds one somewhat of the snow in our streets when a thaw has set in, and the virgin whiteness has given place to dull hues and streaks of filth: but yet in the tinge of blue there is something very beautiful; it is quite cerulean, and the glacier, on closer inspection, discloses a number of clefts or enormous gashes where this color is predominant, and in connection with the shapes in which the ice is thus disposed, produces a very interesting effect. In some cases there are noble caverns formed in the ice; a noted one in Grindelwald some summers since has disappeared, so changeful is the state of these great frozen masses. A walk over the glacier, or rather, as on some parts it proves, a climb or scramble over its blocks of ice, and a careful creeping round the edges of its chasms, give a very different impression from a view at a distance; then one gets at the poetry of the glacier. This is especially the case when the traveler reaches the Mer de Glace, in the vale of Chamouni, under the shadow of Mont Blanc. Looking close upon it from the elevation of Montanvert, or crossing its broad surface toward the Jardin, you are surrounded by a scene which baffles description. The glacier is like a broad river, or arm of the sea, frozen at the instant of its being agitated by the wind, and thrown into irregular billows and contending currents. It lies in a vast hollow among the mountains, and on descending to its surface, it is found broken up by enormous gaps, irregular hillocks, and channels scooped out by the melted snow. The effect of the dirty streaks is lost when a person is toiling along over the ice, and the lofty rocks all round, and the snowy domes and pinnacles beyond, and the silence and the solitude, are perfectly entrancing. To minds of sensibility and imagination, a visit to the Mer de Glace is an era in their history.

So much for the poetry of the glacier. The science of it is not less interesting, though in another way; the glacier is ever in motion, slow but certain motion, and the dirty streaks we have spoken of are what have been called *moraines*, that is, accumulations of stone and rubbish disintegrated from the rocks by the ice in its ceaseless progress toward the valley. These moraines are in ridges running along the sides, and also along the middle of the glacier; hence called *lateral* and *medial* moraines. The formation of the lateral moraines may be understood at a glance; that of the medial is not so obvious, but it becomes plain enough, when it is remembered that the ice sea, if we may so call it, is supplied by tributary streams joining the main body, which also bring with them their moraines formed at the sides, and these meeting in the middle of the Mer de Glace, of course form moraines there. The scientific name of the clefts or openings is *crevasses*, and these are produced by the unequal movement of the glacier, and the influence of sun and wind; great blocks of stone or boulders are found here and there resting on a frozen pedestal, a phenomenon produced by the melting of the snow and ice around the fragment, while the portion on which it rests has been preserved in the shade and screened from the rays of the sun. The glacier on the edge next the valley is ever melting and disappearing, and here, too, cataracts come dashing down, formed of melting snow, constituting the source of rivers —the Arve and the Arveron, for example, in the valley of Chamouni—yet the waste is being ever supplied from the snowy heights, which are constantly yielding material for the formation of ice.

We have spoken of the motion of the glacier; the nature of that motion, for the best theory of which we are indebted to Professor Forbes, must be briefly explained. According to that eminently scientific man, the glacier does not *slide* as was once supposed, but it *flows.* From his observations it appears to be a mass of viscous matter—a body, though of great consistency, yet really fluid; it passes along a very unequal channel; it expands and contracts according to its boundaries; from a broad basin it presses through more limited openings, and the motion of the middle part is less slow than that of its sides; thus it clearly obeys all the laws of fluid motion, and must therefore be considered fluid, though of immense consistency and thickness.

The following striking passage (Forbes's Travels throught the Alps, p. 386) will form a conclusion to this account of glaciers:—" Poets and philosophers have delighted to compare the course of human life to that of a river; perhaps a still fitter simile might be found in the history of a glacier. Heaven-descending in its origin, it yet takes it mold and conformation from the hidden womb of the mountains which brought it forth. At first soft and ductile, it acquires a character and firmness of its own, as an inevitable destiny urges it on its onward career. Jostled and constrained by the crosses and inequalities of its prescribed path, hedged in by impassable barriers which fix limits to its movements, it yields, groaning, to its fate, and still travels forward, seamed with the scars of many a conflict with opposing obstacles; all this while, although wasting, it is renewed by an unseen power; it evaporates but is not consumed. On its surface it bears the spoils which, during the progress of its existence, it has made its own; often weighty burdens, devoid of beauty and value; at times precious masses, sparkling with gems or with ore. Having at length attained its greatest width and extension, commanding admiration by its beauty and power, waste predominates over supply; the vital springs begin to fail; it stoops into an attitude of decrepitude; it drops the burdens one by one, which it had borne so proudly aloft—its dissolution is inevitable. But as it is resolved into its elements, it takes all at once a new, and livelier, and disembarrassed form; from the wreck of its members it arises another, yet the same; a noble, full-bodied, arrowy stream, which leaps rejoicing over the obstacles which before had stayed its progress, and hastens through fertile valleys toward a freer existence, and a final union in the ocean with the boundless and the indefinite."

We may add, that over man as over the glacier there rules a divine law; the agency of God is universal. "He giveth snow like wool: he scattereth the hoar-frost like ashes. He casteth forth his ice like morsels: who can stand before his cold? He sendeth out his word and melteth them: he causeth his wind to blow, and the waters flow. He showeth his word unto Jacob, his statutes and his judgments unto Israel."* Nor should it be forgotten, that only the life which by the renewing grace of God becomes a spiritual one, can be compared to the melted glacier in the latter part of this noble passage. 'T is only when heavenly love, under the renewing influences of the Holy Spirit, melts the frozen soul, that it assumes its new, livelier, and disembarrassed form, and hastens to a freer existence.

The rivers and cataracts of Switzerland require a particular notice. The principal valleys, which form such beautiful features in Swiss scenery, have been scooped out by the rich and sparkling mountain streams which are seen flowing through them, and which swell in their onward course till some of them become deep navigable floods, bearing on their bosom the riches of commerce, and the children of pleasure. The Saane, which rises on the borders of the Valais canton among the Alps, and flows through the valley which bears its name; the Gross Emmen, which begins near the

* Dr. Alexander makes the same remark in his Letters on Switzerland.

Lake of Brienz, and continues below Soleure, and has also a valley of its own; the Reuss, which descends from St. Gothard, making a magnificent fall near Andermatt, and, like the two former, distinguishing by its own appellation the ravine along which it bends its course; and the Limmat, which comes from the Alps of Glarus, through the Lake of Wallenstadt—these are all affluents of the river Aar. That again has its own valley; and after rushing from its birthplace in the glaciers of the Grimsel, and taking its stupendous Handek leap of more than two hundred feet, it winds on to the Lake of Thun, and then round the foot of Berne, and afterward by the base of the Jura. The Saane joins it below Berne; the Gross Emmen below Soleure; the Reuss, near Windesch; the Limmat, a little lower down. The Aar, fed by these affluents, indeed the great drainer of Switzerland, is itself an affluent, and pours its waters into the Rhine at a short distance from Waldshut. The Thur, which rises in the Toggenburg, in the canton of St. Gall, is another tributary of the Rhine, joining it near Rheinau. But it is impossible to enumerate all the smaller contributions which are made to that majestic flow of waters; for as many as two thousand five hundred mountain streams are absorbed by it in its early course. The Rhine itself rises in the

Alps of the Grisons; its two main springs meet at Reichenau, a most pleasant village, where the confluence presents a beautiful picture. On it rolls to Constance, and then beyond Schaffhausen it dashes over the great rocks, there forming the sublime Rhein falls; the grandest in point of breadth, the sublimest in point of volume, and the most beautiful in point of its bank scenery and little rural accessories, of all the falls of Switzerland. To see it on a bright morning, when it looks like a stream of clouds, arched by a rainbow, pressing between its rocky gates, is a sight about which words can say little, but silent pictured thoughts must ever after remain its precious memorial. The banks of the Rhine between Schaffhausen and Basle are exceedingly beautiful, and here and there—near Luffengburg, for example—views are opened of river scenery which may well entrance an artist or a poet. The other great Swiss river is the Rhone; rising at the foot of Mount Furca, and flowing through the broad valley, it receives a number of tributaries, among which may be mentioned the Dala, the Usen, and the Trient. The Rhone flows through the Lake of Geneva, at the west end of which it is joined by the Arve, where is presented the singular phenomenon noticed by all travelers of the two rivers—the Rhone blue as the sky, the Arve brown as the earth—flowing on side by side, touching one another, but not mingling their streams. The scenery of the Rhone is far inferior to that of the Rhine; the broad valley of the former, indeed, is lined by majestic mountains, which cannot but yield magnificent views, and some of the first glimpses of this valley are very imposing, as seen, for instance, from the mountains above Martigny, or from the rocks by the side of the Dala. But the very breadth of the valley lessens the interest of the scenery when the traveler is in the midst of it, and the wide shingly shores when the river is low are a very great drawback upon its effect on a tourist. The valley is an unwholesome region, and it is in this locality that the goitre and cretinism prevail—those terrible scourges of Switzerland; the former an unwieldy protuberance in the neck, the other a most distressing form of idiocy. "Various theories have been resorted to, to account for the goitre: some have attributed it to the use of water derived from melting snow; others to the habit of carrying heavy weights; others again to filthy habits; while a fourth theory derives it from the nature of the soil, or the use of spring water impregnated with calcareous matter." Dr. Forbes rejects the water theory, and inclines to think that the dirty habits of the people may minister to the disease; but he also assigns the *miasma* of the regions where it prevails as a principal cause. It is difficult to trace the connection between the neck swelling and the mental imbecility; but the two maladies certainly coëxist to a remarkable degree in the same localities. We may add, that in many other Swiss valleys these forms of disease are found.

We have only mentioned the rivers which flow *through* Switzerland, but there are other rivers taking their rise on the eastern side of the Alps, the Ticino and Adda, which flow into Italy, and the Juri, which waters the Tyrol. Some of the cataracts of Switzerland have been mentioned in connection with the course of the rivers, but there are others of note that should not be passed over. The Reichenbach, in the vale of Meyringen, is very beautiful, shooting down like a discharge of rockets reversed, and displaying at certain times an iris, like a sun ray, crossing clouds of many-colored dust. The Staubach is another wonderful mountain stream, leaping from its upper bed down into the valley of Lauterbrun, a depth of nine hundred feet, making altogether a thin waving column of water, which becomes mere spray at the lower end. The Giesbach, on the lake of Brienz, is a succession of falls with many beautiful adjuncts in the way of rock and wood: and the Pélérin, in the vale of Chamouni, is a singular cascade, which, falling upon a basin in a rock, makes a fresh leap in the form of a curve, or "parabolic arch of singular beauty." But cascades are plentiful in Switzerland, and it would be vain to attempt their enumeration.

In connection with these scenes, exquisitely lovely or overwhelmingly grand, the traveler is often reminded of terrible catastrophes which have occurred through the overflow of rivers. The following account of one, though rather long, we shall, from its interesting character, venture to insert:—

"In the spring of 1818, the people of the valley of Bagnes became alarmed on observing the low state of the waters of the Drance, at a season when the melting of the snows usually enlarged the torrent; and this alarm was increased by the records of similar appearances before the dreadful inundation of 1595, which was then occasioned by the accumulation of the waters behind the debris of a glacier that formed a dam, which remained until the pressure of the water burst the dike, and it rushed through the valley, leaving desolation in its course. In April, 1818, some persons went up the valley to ascertain the cause of the deficiency of water, and they discovered that vast masses of the glaciers of Getroz, and avalanches of snow had fallen into a narrow part of the valley, between Mont Pleureur and Mont Mauvoisin, and formed a dike of ice and snow six hundred feet wide and four hundred feet high, on a base of three thousand feet, behind which the waters of the Drance had accumulated and formed a lake above seven thousand feet long. M. Venetz, the engineer of the Valais, was consulted, and he immediately decided upon cutting a gallery through this barrier of ice, sixty feet above the level of the water at the time of commencing, and where the dike was six hundred feet thick. He calculated upon making a tunnel through this mass before the water should have risen sixty feet higher in the lake. On the 10th of May, the work was begun by gangs of fifty men, who relieved each other and worked without intermission, day and night, with inconceivable courage and perseverance, neither deterred by the dayly-occurring danger from the falling of fresh masses of the glacier, nor by the rapid increase of the water in the lake, which rose sixty-two feet in thirty-four days—on an average, nearly two feet each day; but it once rose five feet in one day, and threatened each moment to burst the dike by its increasing pressure; or, rising in a more rapid proportion than the men could proceed with their work, render their efforts abortive by rising above them. Sometimes dreadful noises were heard, as the pressure of water detached masses of ice from the bottom, which, floating, presented so much of their bulk above the water as led to the belief that some of them were seventy feet thick. The men persevered in their fearful duty without any serious accident, and, though suffering severely from cold and wet, and surrounded by dangers which cannot be justly described, by the 4th of June they had accomplished an opening six hundred feet long; but having begun their work on both sides of the dike at the same time, the place where they ought to have met was twenty feet lower on one side of the lake than on the other: it was fortunate that latterly the increase of the perpendicular height of the water was less, owing to the extension of its surface. They proceeded to level the highest side of the tunnel, and completed it just before the water reached them. On the evening of the 13th the water began to flow. At first, the opening was not large enough to carry off the supplies of water which the lake received, and it rose two feet above the tunnel; but this soon enlarged from the action of the water, as it melted the floor of the gallery, and the torrent rushed through. In thirty-two hours the lake sank ten feet, and during the following twenty-four hours twenty feet more; in a few days it would have been emptied; for the floor melting, and being driven off as the water escaped, kept itself below the level of the water within; but the cataract which issued from the gallery melted and broke up also a large portion of the base of the dike which had served as its buttress: its resistance decreased faster than the pressure of the lake lessened, and at four o'clock in the afternoon of the 16th of June the dike burst, and in half an hour the water escaped through the breach, and left the lake empty.

"The greatest accumulation of water had been eight hundred million of cubic feet; the tunnel, before the disruption, had carried off nearly three hundred and thirty million—Escher says, two hundred and seventy million; but he neglected to add sixty million which flowed into the lake in three days.

"In half an hour, five hundred and thirty million cubic feet of water passed through the breach, or three hundred thousand feet per second; which is five times greater in quantity than the waters of the Rhine at Basle, where it is one thousand three hundred English feet wide. In one hour and a half the water reached Martigny, a distance of eight leagues. Through the first seventy thousand feet it passed with the velocity of thirty-three feet per second—four or five times faster than the most rapid river known; yet it was charged with ice, rocks, earth, trees, houses, cattle, and men; thirty-four persons were lost, four hundred cottages swept away, and the damage done in the two hours of its desolating power exceeded a million of Swiss livres. All the people of the valley had been cautioned against the danger of a sudden eruption; yet it was fatal to so many. All the bridges in its course were swept away, and among them the bridge of Mauvoisin, which was elevated ninety feet above the ordinary height of the Drance. If the dike had remained untouched, and it could have endured the pressure until the lake had reached the level of its top, a volume of seventeen hundred million cubic feet of water would have been accumulated there, and a devastation much more fatal and extensive must have been the consequence. From this greater danger, the people of the valley of the Drance were preserved by the heroism and devotion of the brave men who effected the formation of the gallery over the dike, under the direction of M. Venetz. We know no instance on record of courage equal to this; their risk of life was not for fame or for riches—they had not the usual excitements to personal risk in a world's applause or gazetted promotion—their devoted courage was to save the lives and property of their fellow-men, not to destroy them. They steadily and heroically persevered in their labors, amid dangers such as a field of battle never presented, and from which some of the bravest men, of mere animal courage, who ever lived, would have shrunk in dismay. These truly brave Vallaisians deserve all honor."

We must now add a few words in reference to the Swiss lakes. The largest of these is Lake Leman, or the Lake of Geneva. It is about forty-seven miles in length, measuring it as nearly as possible in a straight line. Pen and pencil have often been employed in portraying its scenery, but neither has sufficed to do justice to its charms. The western end by Geneva and the opposite end by Vevay are very different; each, however, possessing an aspect of peculiar interest. The old city of Geneva washing its foot in the clear blue waters, and the gently-sloping banks as the lake widens toward the east, and the numerous villas and gardens which speckle and variegate the shores, and the far-distant view of Mont Blanc and the whole of the majestic range of neighboring mountains which you catch to the south, are objects which, when seen on a clear sunny day, more than realize the poetic dreams created beforehand by description. Vevay partly touching the water-side and partly perched on a hill, with the Castle of Chillon not far off, and the amphitheater of mountains rising rather abruptly from the edge of the lake, and shutting in the scene, form a fine contrast to what is seen at the other end. But it is only the contrast which obtains between one form of beauty and another. The boats scudding over the lake in full sail, or slowly plied by oars, or resting quietly in their own shadow, filled perhaps with gayly-dressed peasants, or rich market stores of fruits and vegetables, add very greatly to the effect of the general picture. Persons of intelligence while traversing this region will remember certain names with which the shores are associated. The forms of Voltaire, and Rousseau, and Gibbon, and Byron, will come before the imagination; but though the genius of these men will give interest to the spots where they trod, the perversion of that genius, the frightful employment of it on the side of infidelity and vice, will throw a dark moral shadow over their homes and haunts—the only thing which there is on Lake Leman, judging by our own experience, to diminish the rich deep pleasure of a visit. The Lake of Constance, forty-four miles in length, is next to Leman in point of size, but far inferior in point of scenery, though its shores, generally flat and tame, are not without some picturesque points. Neuchâtel comes next in reference to extent, being twenty-five miles long, and though, like Constance, it can never vie with some of its sisters in this land of lakes, yet "the glorious view of the Alps from the heights of the Jura above the town must appear magnificent; and should the sky be clear, and the traveler's temper even, the object around will assume a different aspect, and Neuchâtel, with its picturesque old castle, its numerous white country houses, its vine-clad hills, and its blue expanse of lake, will be pronounced beautiful." The lake of the four cantons is about the same length as Neuchâtel, but its form is very different; the latter being straight, the former bent into four branches like the arms of a star-fish, the arm to the east being greatly lengthened out and angularly bent in the direction of Altorf. What Ullswater is to Windermere, the lake of the Waldstatter is to Neuchâtel, and more—for no Cumberland scenery can match the glories of Switzerland, especially in this locality. We give the preference to the Waldstatter over all the other lakes. The view from Luzern across the blue waters, taking in the Righi and Pilatus, and the magnificent ranges of many-colored mountains tipped with snow; and then the connected views as the traveler in a boat passes from one headland to another, and looks down the beautiful creeks or inlets which successively open—while the shores become more precipitous, till toward the east end they shoot up from the water's edge in steep declivities—are wonderfully enchanting: the first so soothing, the second so heart-stirring. The associations of the latter are in harmony. Hereabouts is the Tell region, approaching toward Altorf, the scene of the apple-shooting; there lies on the right the green slope of Rutli, the trysting place of all the Swiss patriots, at the foot of a lofty mountain; there stands on the left the little chapel, among clustering rocks and trees, which was built in commemoration of Tell's escape from Gessler. But our space forbids us to enlarge, and we must hastily notice the other lakes. Zurich is twenty-four miles long, and a truly pleasant region it is, calm and cheerful as gently-sloping banks and busy villages can make it. The smaller lakes are Thun, Brienz, Zug, Bienne, and Morat. The last has little to recommend it; the fourth, anywhere but in Switzerland, would be noticeable for beauty; the first three even there have claims on the traveler's admiration.

And now, in closing this chapter on nature as seen in Switzerland, one feels the truth of the sentiment expressed by Arnold when in Italy:— "Truly may one feel with Von Canitz, that if the glory of God's perishable works be so great, what must be the glory of the imperishable—what infinitely more of him who is the Author of both? And if I feel thrilling through me the sense of this outward beauty, innocent indeed, yet necessarily unconscious, what is the sense one ought to have of moral beauty, of God, thé Holy Spirit's creation, of humbleness and truth, self-devotion and love! Much more beautiful, because made truly after God's image, are the forms and colors of kind, and wise, and holy thoughts, and words and actions; more truly beautiful is one hour of old Mrs. Price's* patient waiting for the Lord's time, and her cheerful and kind interest in us all, as if she owed us anything, than this glorious valley of the Velinus; for this will pass away, and that will not pass away. But that is not the great point: believe with Aristotle that this should abide, and that should perish; still there is in the moral beauty an inherent excellence which the natural beauty cannot have. His living and conscious ministers and servants are, it is permitted us to say, the temples of which the light is God himself." And if these thoughts apply to the experience and manifestation of piety in the

* An old woman in the almshouse at Rugby.

heart, how much more do they apply to that truth—that divine, and blessed, and glorious truth which paints the colors of holy thought, and which God employs as the means of building up the spiritual temple of his presence on earth! Inspired truth must be placed by us above all the scenery of nature. It has majesty more majestic than the mountain, strength more enduring than Mont Blanc, purity whiter than the snow, brightness more piercing than the sunlit waters, and beauty sweeter far than the Alpine rose. Let this thought be our companion in every ramble amid natural scenery, and while we enjoy the lesser, let us not lose the benefit of the greater gift. Let reflections, gathered from God's book, blend with the observation of God's work; and let us rise from the adoring love of God in creation, to the filial and trustful love of God in Christ.

CHAPTER II.

ART.

We shall begin with some account of the towns and buildings of Switzerland. There is not much artistically beautiful in the architecture of Switzerland, yet there is in its edifices something of interest to the antiquary and the lover of the picturesque. In connection with our notice of buildings, we shall touch on their historical associations. We greatly like old Zurich, with its antique-fashioned houses, and its later accessions of mansions, and villas, and hotels. The rather handsome Church of St. Peter will be visited, more for the sake of its connection with Lavater—who was its minister, and who was shot by a French soldier at his own door—than for its architectural pretensions. The massive rauthaus, of modern erection, with its memorials outside of Swiss heroes, will detain the stranger a little while as he reads the inscriptions; but the chief object of interest to one of architectural and archæological taste will .e the cathedral or minster, on the left bank of the Limmat. It belongs to the large division of Romanesque architecture which we style Lombardic, and which, in many of its features and details, reminds us much of the Saxon and Norman. Its most characteristic parts are, as to the exterior of the buildings, the two towers at the west end; the highly ornamental doorway on the north side, in the Lombard style, with pointed insertions; and the cloisters, now a playground for schoolboys, which exhibit rows of round-headed arches, and many curious enrichments at the top of the small pillars. The designs are in some cases very odd and grotesque; and it amuses one to trace here Delilah cutting off Samson's locks, and there, wolves attacking a hog, or a bear carrying off a pig in triumph. As to the inside of the church, it presents Norman-like arches with plain capitals, and a triforium turned into a gallery. The choir is now parted off from the nave, and the latter is used as the place for worship. Of course one thinks of Zwingle at Zurich; and having pictured him in this old church, proclaiming the doctrines of salvation by grace through faith, while crowds were hanging on his lips to hear the good old doctrine—to them, however, as new as it was refreshing—it is interesting to visit the house where it is said he lived, now a mere relic, of conventual appearance.

Basle is remarkable for the Swiss aspect of its houses on the one side of the town, and the German character of them on the other. The rauthaus is Gothic, of the date 1508, and there is a handsome hospital of modern age on the site of the palace of the margraves of Baden. The old gateways are highly interesting, with flanking towers, machicolations, and portcullis, all well preserved; and the fountains in the streets look very cool and pleasant on a hot summer's day. But the chief object of interest is the minster at the top of the hill on the west bank of the Rhine.

So deep is the color of the red sandstone of which it is built, that it looks as if it had been ochered all over. It was begun when so many other churches were built in the eleventh century, though the oldest part now remaining is of the twelfth. There are two towers on the west front, and two equestrian statues worth looking at. The portal of the north transept is worthy of special attention, and down in the crypt under the church are some very ancient relics of architecture and sculpture, perhaps as old as the foundation of the edifice. The chapter-house and the cloisters are very remarkable; the one for its having been occupied by the fathers of the Council of Basle, the other for having been probably a place of resort for Erasmus, who latterly lived and at last died in the town. Œcolampadius, and Grynaus, and Meyer are buried here. Erasmus also lies entombed in the church, whose high-built pews block up the place of his sepulcher. The oldest church in Basle is St. Martin's, where Œcolampadius used to preach. Connected with the University of Basle, which occupies a range of modern buildings very fresh and white, are the famous library and museum—the former enriched by numerous MSS., and the latter containing a fine collection of paintings and drawings by Holbein. Holbein lived in Basle, the chief association with

Switzerland of any very eminent name in the history of the fine arts. Many of his productions here are very original and characteristic; and a curious story is told of him, more creditable to his skill in foreshortening than to his moral habits. He painted a pair of legs so well that, putting them on a scaffold by a window, the person inside thought that the painter was at work, when in fact he was far otherwise employed at a neighboring wine-shop.

A room in the house of the Rev. J. Linder, Archdeacon of Basle, is that assigned by tradition as the chamber where Œcolampadius died. "Opposite the door of entrance to this room," says Dr. Alexander,* "are two windows; on the left hand the wall is pierced by a door, on the right the wall is unbroken from end to end. Against the latter wall, I judge, was placed the couch of Œcolampadius, and at these windows entered those morning rays amid which his spirit passed away. It is a brave and hallowed story, that of the death-bed scene of Œcolampadius. As night gathered, and the rumor spread that the reformer would not live till the morning, the ministers of Basle, to the number of ten, hastened to his presence. Already, on a former occasion, he had given them his dying charge, beseeching them to

* Dr. Alexander on the Swiss Churches.

be men of light and men of love; now he said but little, as he desired to remain calm and still. 'Do you bring any tidings?' exclaimed he to a person of rank who entered the room. The answer was in the negative. A feeling of self-reproach seemed to cross his mind for asking such a question at such a moment, and he said hastily, 'But I—I shall soon be with my Lord.' By and by, one asked him whether the light of the lamp did not annoy him. Laying his hand on his heart, he exclaimed, 'Here, here is where I have enough of light.' At length the day began to dawn; in a feeble voice he chanted the fifty-first psalm; and then heaving a sigh, he said, 'Lord Jesus, come to my help.' He spoke no more, but quietly breathed his last. The sun now poured his rays into the chamber; but they fell on that inanimate corpse, and on the pale and weeping friends, who, with uplifted hands, were kneeling around his couch. Does it not seem striking that one who, answerable to his name, had been such 'a bright and shining light' in the world, should, in the last words he addressed to his fellow-men, have spoken so firmly and joyously of that light which was within him—a light in which thousands had rejoiced to walk, and which calumny has not been able to darken, nor death itself to extinguish? Striking, too, that one whose life had been a long and earnest protest against darkness, should thus wait for the morning light ere he passed away to be forever with Him who dwelleth in light, and in whom there is no darkness at all!"

Berne is finely situated on the top of a promontory formed by the winding of the Aar, which is here crossed by a noble bridge. The town sits like a mural crown on the brow of the hill. Very curious are some of the streets of Berne, the pavement by the shops on each side being inclosed under heavy arcades, which give the place somewhat of an eastern look. The clock tower, the cage tower, and the Christopher tower in the principal street, are very odd grotesque-looking edifices, with their great ugly paintings and droll clock-work puppets. Bears sculptured in different orders of merit constitute favourite ornaments in Berne, in honor of their founder, and till of late live bears have been kept by the Aarburg gate. The museum, containing specimens of stuffed animals and other natural curiosities, is a place in which to spend a few hours pleasurably and with instruction. "Berne is celebrated for the number and excellence of its charitable institutions; they are perhaps more carefully attended to than any in Europe. There is a public granary in case of scarcity, two orphan houses, an infirmary, and an extensive hospital, bearing the inscription '*Christo in pauperibus.*' It was for a long time the finest, indeed the only grand building in the town, a just subject of gratification; but it has of late been eclipsed by the colossal dimensions of the new prison and penitentiary, a circumstance characteristic of the present period perhaps in other countries besides the canton of Berne." The principal building is the cathedral, a fine Gothic building of the fifteenth century, considered to have been planned by the architect of Strasburg minster. Everybody, on entering it at the west end, must notice the sculpture of the last judgment over the principal doorway, one of those illustrations of the *theology* of mediæval art which are very curious, showing the gross ideas of Scriptural subjects then prevalent, and how much something was needed to raise the tone of religious thought, to spiritualize ideas of the future state, and to detach the awful from the grotesque. The carving in the choir is worth examination, and the painted windows are very remarkable for subjects as well as style; for in one there is the pope grinding the four evangelists in a mill, whence there comes a stream of wafers, which a bishop is busy in gathering into his chalice. In the chancel part there are preserved some of the rich tapestry and coverings which were seized in the camp of Charles of Burgundy, at Morat. The platform on which the church stands, on the river side, is a work of art, for it is supported by a massive wall of masonry one hundred and eight feet high. The houses studding the side of the hill down to the lower part of the town remind one of some parts of Clifton, near Bristol. It is recorded that a spirited horse, with a young student on his back, was once frightened by some children, and leaped down from the platform to the base of the precipice, with no other injury than a few broken ribs; and that the student lived to a good old age, clergyman of the parish of Kerzerz. The view of the Aar and the country beyond, with the distant Alps, forms the chief attraction of the platform, an advantage which is augmented if the traveler ascends to the top of the cathedral: there is one of the noblest prospects in Switzerland.

As specimens of the fine arts are not very numerous in Switzerland, we will venture here to insert, from the interesting work of Archdeacon Coxe, an account of a piece of sculpture at Hindelbank, a village about four miles from Berne, executed by Nahl, a Saxon sculptor. "Being employed in constructing a sepulcher for Count d'Erlach, he was lodged in the house of the clergyman, his particular friend, whose wife, a woman of uncommon beauty, expired in childbed on Easter-eve. Struck with the time of her death, animated by the recollection of her beauty, sympathizing with the affliction of her husband she conceived and finished this affecting monument. It is placed in the body of the church, sunk into the pavement like a grave, and covered with two folding doors: when these are opened, a gravestone appears, as if just rent into three fractures, through which is half discovered the figure of a woman slightly vailed with a shroud. She is represented at the moment of the resurrection, when the graves are commanded to yield up their dead; her right hand is gently raising that portion of the broken stone which lies over her head, and the other holds a naked infant struggling with its little hands to release itself from the tomb. 'Here am I, Lord, and the children whom thou gavest me,' are the sublime words which form the inscription. Below is the name of the deceased, 'Anna Magdalena Langhams, wife of the clergyman, born 1723, died 1751.' The workmanship is by no means inferior to the original design; the artist has formed the whole sepulcher out of one block, and so naturally expressed the swelling of the stone, that the fragments seem as if they had just burst, and were in the act of opening. The only circumstance to be regretted is, that the materials are not so durable as such a monument deserves; being of sand-stone, they are too soft to resist the effects of time, and even now exhibit some symptoms of decay."

Luzern has no remarkable buildings; the Church of St. Leger, the principal one, has nothing to recommend it, though, indeed, the quaint monuments in the cloisters may be worth inspection. The covered bridges are the chief structures of interest; one, the longest of all, has been lately removed. The two which remain are the mill bridge and the upper bridge: the former has on the rafters paintings of the dance of death; the latter, seventy-seven rude designs representing the legendary tales of Luzern's patron saints.

Wordsworth was much interested in these pictures:—

"Long may these homely works devised of old,
These simple efforts of Helvetian skill,
Aid with congenial influence to uphold
The state—the country's destiny to mold;
Turning for them who pass the common dust
Of servile opportunity to gold;
Filling the soul with sentiments august,
The beautiful, the brave, the holy, and the just."*

* These lines now hardly apply, as the Scripture pictures to which he chiefly alludes were in the bridge since destroyed.

It is to be feared, however, that these pictures have not upon the people much of the effect desired by the poet; for, except tourists, nobody looks at them. These bridges, it may be remarked, together with the pictures on the walls of the houses, and the elevated range of watch-towers behind the town, give it an unusually picturesque appearance.

But the great lion of Luzern is literally a lion—a lion most exquisitely sculptured in bold relief on the side of the rock near the gate to Weggis. The animal is represented in the agony of death, with a broken spear in his body, and his fore-paw resting on the shield of France. It is a design by Thorwaldsen, and was executed by Ahorn, a sculptor of Constance, to the memory of the unfortunate Swiss who fell during the French revolution in August and September, 1792, as they were defending the Tuileries against the attacks of the mob. A shadow comes over the remembrance of their bravery and fidelity, when it is recollected that they were mercenary troops, engaged in foreign service, and perishing in a cause to which they were attached by mere pay, and not principle. "There is," as it is remarked in Murray's guide-book, "a quiet solitude and shade about the spot, which is particularly pleasing and refreshing. The rocks around are mantled with fern and creepers, forming a natural framework of the monument, and a streamlet of clear water trickling down from the top of the rock is received into a basin shaped hollow below it, forming a mirror in which the sculpture is reflected. One of the very few survivors of the Swiss guard, dressed in its red uniform, used to act as guardian of the monument, and cicerone to the stranger; but it is believed that the last of this brave band is now dead." The arsenal contains some military antiquities and trophies, and among works of art in Luzern must be included the model of Switzerland by General Pfyffer.

Fribourg, in its fortifications, affords forms of feudal military art in its watch-towers and gateways, and specimens of ancient domestic architecture in some of its houses; altogether the town has a very romantic air. The Church of St. Nicholas is a Gothic building, commenced in the thirteenth century and finished in 1500. The portal under the tower exhibits a sculpture of the last judgment, in the grossest of that style of theological art before noticed. The organ in the church is of world-wide fame; but the chief objects of art at Fribourg are the bridges. The suspension bridge, the longest of a single curve in the world, extends to the length of nine hundred and forty-one feet, and is at an elevation of one hundred and eighty feet,* and in height one hundred and thirty. Four iron cables support the bridge, and these enter the ground obliquely, and are carried down into shafts cut out of the rock. It is all of Swiss production; the iron was from Berne, the lime-stone from the Jura, and the wood from neighboring forests, while every workman, except one, was a native; the heaviest weights produce scarcely a vibration in this ingenious structure. On the opposite side of the river there is another suspension bridge, six hundred and forty feet long, even more curious than the other. Three miles from Fribourg is the grotto of St. Magdalene, cut out of the sandstone by one person in the course of ten years.

Geneva is the largest town in Switzerland, and has in it more of bustle than any other. The quay and upper part contain some very fine modern houses—the rest is old-fashioned, and bears some resemblance to old Edinburgh. The museum, library, and post-office, are the chief public buildings, but none of them are at all noticeable. The cathedral would not be a bad building if it were not for the Corinthian portico absurdly placed in front of what is Lombardic, and that of

* The Menai bridge is only five hundred and eighty feet long.

the simplest and severest style. The interior has been restored, and is a very good specimen of its order and style. Here Calvin preached, and of him there is a memorial on the canopy over the pulpit; the same beneath which his voice often resounded. There is a house, said to have been inhabited by him, in the Rue de Chanoines, but on inquiry we found the tradition to be very apocryphal. He is buried in the cemetery of the Plain Palais, but, according to his wish, his grave remains without a monument. Rousseau was born in Geneva; but a far more pleasing association to our mind is found in the fact, that here some of our countrymen found refuge at the time of the Reformation, and that here was prepared the famous translation of the Bible called the Genevan version, so much prized by our Puritan ancestors. Near Geneva is Ferney, where Voltaire lived; his house, not at all uncommon in itself, is suggestive of very painful thoughts to a Christian mind as having been the abode of such a man. There is in the garden a very pleasant walk, under a covering of clipped hornbeam, on the side of which there are gaps cut to allow a view of the distant prospect. Here it was that the great literary infidel used to saunter and dictate, insensible to the love of that Being who has spread around this spot so much of the beautiful and the grand—deaf to the voice of his Divine Son, without whom "nothing was made that is made," and, still more awful, inspired by intense enmity to that only name, given under heaven, whereby we must be saved.

Lausanne is a considerable town on the shores of Lake Leman, built on a slope in a series of steps. The castle and the cathedral are the principal edifices; the former a square tower with turrets, the latter the finest Gothic church in Switzerland. There are groined arches behind the altar, apparently belonging to the eleventh century, but the present building almost entirely dates from the year 1275. In spite of the present arrangements, formed by closing up the choir and removing the stalls, the interior is still very beautiful, and affords valuable materials for architect ural studies. The grouping of columns, and the style and method of the arches, are very peculiar. The church contains a monument of Otho of Granson, and the tomb of Victor Amadeus VIII., who was Duke of Savoy and Bishop of Geneva, and afterward pope, under the title of Felix V. It was at Lausanne that Gibbon lived; there he wrote the latter part of "The Decline and Fall of the Roman Empire." Some Roman antiquities found in the neighborhood are preserved at Lausanne, including an altar of white marble, and a milestone bearing the name of Antoninus Pius, who was a great benefactor to the ancient Helvetians.

There are other towns in Switzerland of the smaller class, not requiring very particular notice. Soleure is interesting for what still remains of its fortifications, and for its old clock tower. Neuchâtel contains an old church and castle, and a modern hotel de ville and gymnasium. Constance is very antique, and contains several houses of the fifteenth century, and is especially memorable for its connection with John Huss, who was burned in the neighborhood of the town, through an infamous breach of faith, as well as a cruel exercise of tyranny on the part of the council which met here in 1414. St. Gall still retains some considerable portion of its famous abbey, alluded to in a former part of this work. Zug has one or two worth looking into, and a traveler passing through it should by all means stop to glance at the bone-house connected with one at the back of the town, where a number of skulls are ranged in rows, all polished and labelled, bearing the names of the persons they belonged to, and the date of their death: the date of some of them being very recent. Thun is a very picturesque old town, and is remarkable for its tower and church, situated on the very summit of the hill on which the town stands, and giving to it a singularly conical appearance. The streets with their raised galleries over lower shops will, perhaps, remind the tourist of the city of Chester, in England; and he will do well to ramble up into the churchyard, and look down on the prospect of mountain and flood.

Vevay is another small town, with a church and churchyard at the top of a hill; but here the hill lies behind the town, and there slumber in it the remains of General Ludlow, one of the celebrated characters connected with the commonwealth. His monument is a plain grave-stone of black marble.

Stanz, Sarneu, Altorf, and Schwyz, in the Waldstätte, as well as some other still smaller towns in other parts, must be passed over with the remark, that the buildings in them are very simple, and their whole appearance indicates the unambitious taste and the quiet and rural habits of the people.

We have spoken of houses in the town; the houses in the country also deserve a passing remark. But they need no particular description here, because every one is familiar with the ingenious and accurate models of them sold in our toy-shops. The galleries, projecting roofs, and green windows are exceedingly picturesque, especially as seen on the sides of the mountains or embowered among the trees. They often have large stones placed on the roofs to preserve them against the wind; and in the canton of Berne you frequently see inscriptions in German on the front of these dwellings, consisting of passages of Scripture and the names of the persons by whom they were erected. The châlets, so numerous in the upland pasturage, are but mean hovels and cattle-sheds.

Engineering in Switzerland has accomplished some remarkable achievements. Perhaps the most striking displays of practical skill, combined with sound scientific knowledge, are the roads which have been carried over the mountains. They wind in zigzags very curiously up steep ascents. They are carried over immense gulfs and tremendous torrents—

> "The rugged rock
> Opens and lets them in, and on they run,
> Winding their easy way from clime to clime,
> Through glens lock'd up before."

They are often nothing more than shelves cut on the face of the rock sufficiently wide to admit of carriages passing each other. Formerly the main roads, as well as others, were very insecure and imperfectly laid down, wood being sometimes the chief material employed; but modern engineering skill has accomplished great improvements, and for the most part the roads in the Alps of Switzerland are as firm and smooth as the English turnpikes. The principal of the mountain roads are the three great roads into Italy: the Splügen, the St. Gothard, and the Simplon. The last is the work of Napoleon, and was commenced immediately after the battle of Marengo. The engineer was M. Céard, and the whole undertaking was completed in six years, more than thirty thousand men being employed on it at a time. Not less than six hundred and eleven bridges may be numbered in the course of this surprising work of art. Ten galleries are cut for it in the rock or are built of stone, and for miles and miles it is carried over lofty terraces. Sometimes the work is so contrived as to serve the double purpose of viaduct and aqueduct, and, strange as it may seem, it even passes *under* both glacier and waterfall. The gallery of Gondo is five hundred and ninety-six feet long, and it required one hundred workmen day and night for eighteen months to construct it. They not only worked at both ends, but two lateral openings were made by miners suspended by ropes, so that thus they wrought at four points together, and the lateral openings are now made to serve as windows. Opposite one is the simple, but proud inscription, "Ære Italo,

1805, *Nap. Imp.*" The average slope of the road is about six inches in six feet, and the breadth is never less than twenty-five feet. The cost was $25,000 a mile. Houses of refuge are built at intervals, and the whole deserves the eulogium of Sir James Mackintosh: "The Simplon may be safely said to be the most wonderful of useful works; because, though our canals and docks surpass it in utility, science, and magnitude, they have no grandeur to the eye. Its peculiar character is to be the greatest of those monuments that at once dazzle the imagination by their splendor, and are subservient to general convenience." To keep this road throughout in good repair is very expensive, and hence in some part of the Sardinian states it is in a terrible condition, carriages having to be dragged through the beds of torrents. Throughout the whole line accidents are frequently occurring in bad weather, by the bursting of floods and the fall of snow, which break up the path; and, therefore, without constant attention and expense, such a work as this is soon comes to a very ruinous state.

Another instance of engineering in Switzerland, of a different kind, we shall now notice. It is the partial draining of the Lake of Lungern. Every traveler perceives that some strange change has taken place there, for a part of the old bed of the waters is now covered with vegetation, and does credit to the toils of the agriculturist; five hundred acres of good land have been obtained, though certainly at the expense of appearance; for the banks of the lake, in point of scenery, are now quite spoiled. The enterprise was accomplished by a joint-stock company formed of persons in the district, and the engineer employed was Sulzberger. A tunnel was formed near Burglen, carried upward in a sloping direction toward the lake. When the tunnel was brought pretty near the bed of the waters, the difficulty was to prevent a sudden eruption, which might prove very destructive. First, it was determined to bore holes; but the first attempt, though a hole was bored, proved unsuccessful, owing to the nature of the soil. The engineer then determined on forming a mine, and therefore enlarged the end of his tunnel into a chamber six feet square, and within six feet of the lake. Here a charge of powder was placed, and precautions taken to prevent its exploding in the wrong direction. The process was very arduous and full of danger, owing to the foulness of the air and the running in of water; but five hundred men persevered and finished their task. On the 9th of January the explosion took place. The train was fired by three hardy fellows, who employed an enormously long match. Ten minutes after the firing there was a dull explosion, very dubious in report it seemed, so that fears began to be entertained lest the scheme had failed, when suddenly an immense torrent of black mud made its appearance at the lower end of the tunnel. The drainage then went on gradually, and in fourteen days the lake had fallen to the level of the tunnel's mouth. The cost was $25,000, and the whole of the labor was performed by the peasants.

As a further and different illustration of engineering skill, may be noticed an example in the mining department at Bex salt-works, on the Simplon road, between Chillon and St. Maurice. Formerly the brine springs were the only sources from which salt was obtained, and it is interesting to read the following notice of them given by Coxe. It will fully introduce our account of what has subsequently been done here by enterprise and art. "Upon our arrival at the salt springs, I put on a workman's jacket, and went into the mountains about three thousand feet almost horizontally. The gallery is six feet high and four broad, and as much hollowed as if cut with a chisel; it is hewn in a black rock, veined in some places with white gypsum. The salt is procured from springs which are found within a solid rock perforated at great expense; the richest source yields twenty-eight pounds of salt per cent., and the poorest but half a pound. Near these springs are several warm sources, which contain a mixture of salt, but are so strongly impregnated with sulphur as to flame when a lighted candle is put into the pipe through which they flow. After traveling in this subterraneous passage near three-quarters of a mile, I observed a great wheel of thirty-five feet diameter, which raises the brine from the depth of about seventy feet. From this place is a shaft three hundred feet high, which is cut through the mountain to the surface, for the purpose of introducing fresh air. I noticed two reservoirs hollowed in the solid rock for holding the brine; one was one hundred and sixty feet square and nine in depth. Since my first expedition in 1776, the workmen had pierced the rock twenty-five feet deeper, and cut a gallery a hundred feet in length; they had also begun to form a third reservoir, to contain five thousand five hundred cubic feet, which was nearly half finished. The brine deposited in these reservoirs is conveyed by means of two thousand pipes, about a league, to Bexvieux, where the salt is extracted." In 1823, the springs were found to be failing, when M. Charpentier proposed to search for rock salt. Accordingly, shafts and galleries were constructed, and a rich vein was traced to a distance of four thousand feet. The rock salt is blasted with gunpowder, then crushed and thrown into large reservoirs, where it is dissolved. Each reservoir is filled with water three times, the last two solutions being weaker than the first. The brine thus obtained is further subjected to a process of *graduation* in long sheds, where the salt water, raised to the roof by pumps, comes trickling down in drops, thus producing evaporation of the watery particles. The salt crystallizes, and is afterward boiled in pans.

But we must leave these ingenious contrivances to extract wealth from the stores of nature, to afford some account of the manufactures which display so eminently the skill and industry of the Swiss. Switzerland has its iron works in the cantons of Berne, Soleure, and Vaud. At Zurich there is an extensive manufactory of machines belonging to Mr. Escher, and employing seven hundred hands; and every traveler must have noticed many of the iron steamers on the Swiss lakes as having been made at this large establishment. The manufacture of silks in Switzerland is far more important, being one of the main staples of its trade. Twelve or thirteen thousand people are employed upon it in the canton of Zurich, where many of the masters grow rich without much polish, according to the proverb,

"*Grossier comme un Zurichois.*" Six hundred thousand pounds sterling is the produce of the Zurich silk manufactory. "Rarely," observes Dr. Bowring, in his interesting report on Swiss commerce, "are there a number of looms at work collectively; almost all are to be found singly, or two together, seldom even three or four. In the common apartment of the family of the country people, one or two members of the family may be seen weaving, and carrying on at the same time their household occupations; sometimes working in the gardens: other members of the family, even the children when released from school, assist in the winding of the silk; and it is this union of manufacturing with agricultural pursuits which has combined to promote the trade." Silk ribbons, taffetas, and satins, are made in great quantities at Basle, keeping between three and four thousand looms employed, and supplying annual exports to the amount of ten millions of francs. Cotton goods also are largely manufactured in Switzerland; Zurich adding this branch to her silk trade, and having as many as twelve thousand cotton weavers. In the canton of St. Gall and Appenzell, a great deal is done in the same line; the workmen, as in Zurich, dividing their time between the loom and the plow. Schaffhausen has its cotton spinners, and in

Thurgau, Glarus, and Aargau there are various descriptions of cotton cloth produced. Cotton printing is extensively carried on in Neuchâtel, and a considerable amount of it is also executed in the last of the cantons before named. Lace likewise is made at Neuchâtel, though not in such large quantities as formerly. Stockings and hosiery are produced at Aargau. As to hardware, Schaffhausen has a manufactory in high repute for steel and files, and Geneva has its cutlery, so has the canton Vaud: pottery and leather, firearms and saddlery, are also mentioned among Swiss manufactures, especially in Geneva.

But the articles best known among us are the watches of the latter place. One hundred thousand watches are annually made there, employing between thirteen and fourteen hundred workmen; and the shops, which display splendid assortments of these beautiful goods, as well as musical boxes and jewelry, are among the lions of the city visited by tourists. The largest and most celebrated is that of Bautte & Co., Rue du Rhône. "The watches of English manufacture," remarks Dr. Bowring in his report, "do not come into competition with those of Swiss production, which are used for different purposes and by a different class of persons. Notwithstanding all the risks and charges, the sale of Swiss watches is large;

and it has not really injured the English watch-making trade. The English watches are far more solid in construction, fitter for service, and especially in countries where no good watchmakers are to be found, as the Swiss watches require delicate treatment. English watches, therefore, are sold to the purchaser who can pay a high price; the Swiss watches supply the classes to whom a costly watch is inaccessible." In Neuchâtel there is as much of watchmaking now as in Geneva. From one hundred thousand to one hundred and twenty thousand are annually made in that canton, and many a villager among the Jura Mountains obtains his livelihood by this ingenious craft. About a third of the watches are gold, the rest are silver. Some of the latter sell as low as from twenty to twenty-five francs.

Among the characteristic productions of this interesting people, we cannot avoid noticing their wooden toys and ornaments. Every one is familiar with the farm-houses and châlets; the lions, bears, and chamois; the peasant-girls, shepherds, and hunters, so delicately carved. These are chiefly made at Interlachen and Meyringen; at least, there principally we have noticed the manufacture going on, and have been not a little interested as we have stopped to watch the progress of the humble wood-carver. At the doors of cottages, in rooms fitted up for the purpose in hotels, and in considerable shops here and there, these tempting goods are offered for sale to the tourist, who cannot do better than fix on some of these ingenious articles, if he wish to carry away any mementoes of Switzerland. Articles of a very superior order, for useful as well as ornamental purposes—especially tables, richly carved and exquisitely painted—are to be obtained at some of the larger depositories, especially in the shops at Berne; and another pleasing souvenir of Switzerland, at once national and artistic, may be obtained in beautiful collections of dried wild-flowers, arranged in book-like cases, framed according to scientific nomenclature. We were much pleased with some specimens of this *hortus siccus* which we met with at Rosenlau, and brought home with us: it still affords a welcome quickener of memory and imagination when we spread out its treasures of Alpine botany.

To proceed to the subject of agriculture. We do not know whether there be much of science in the Swiss husbandry; but we can answer for the simple art and diligent industry which it displays. The peasant has reclaimed from waste every available spot; and it is interesting to observe the ledges of the rocks laid under cultivation, and rich in cabbages and edible roots. The irrigation of the higher spots on the mountains, which the husbandman has made the scene of his toils, is very laborious; and people may be seen climbing up the steeps with large wooden tubs fastened to their backs full of water. The mountain torrents are also made available for watering the fields, and rude wooden troughs of fir-tree are used for conveying the stream to the desired spot. The Swiss farmers are great economists of manure, and piles of that material are often met with by the side of the road in villages, by no means yielding a fragrant odor. A large portion of Switzerland is used for pasture-land, and in many parts there are rich crops of hay. When at the hay harvest, the women, in the costume of their canton, busily engaged in hay-making, give increased animation to the rural scene. Corn is not cultivated to a great extent, owing to the lofty elevation of the country preventing its growth. Buckwheat is sown successfully at a height of two thousand two hundred feet; maize at two thousand five hundred; barley and rye at four thousand; flax, and hemp, and maize are all reared in the highlands. Carrots, turnips, and cabbages, are planted as high as five thousand feet. Mulberry-trees and silk-worms are reared on the Ticino side of the Alps. Chestnuts, walnuts, olive, fig, and peach-trees, and even pomegranates and almonds are grown in some parts. Cider is made in the highlands, and a drink, distilled from cherries, is common all over Switzerland. Beer is brewed in most of the towns, but of inferior quality, and a good deal of wine is made in the canton of Neuchâtel, some of it resembling Burgundy; sparkling wines are produced at Cortaillod and Auvergnier. In the cantons of Geneva, Zurich, Schaffhausen, Valais, some part of Aargau, Thurgau, St. Gall, and Basle, the vine is very much cultivated: but on the Italian side of Italy the vineyards are richest, and they form an object of beauty by the road-side, as they spread out in a field of rich foliage trained over supporters, so as to form a series of embowered alleys and vistas.

CHAPTER III.

SOCIETY.

We have already intimated our intention to notice briefly the forms of the cantonal governments in Switzerland. Most of them are representative. Some require a property qualification in the electors. This is the case in Luzern, Ticino, and Geneva. A still higher qualification is required for members of the legislative chamber. In Luzern, persons are admissible to the council at twenty-five years of age. At Ticino, they are not eligible for that dignity till they are thirty. Both there and at Geneva the elective franchise is confined to those who are twenty-five and upward. In most of the cantons having a representative government, the suffrage is universal. It is so in Berne, Zurich, Vaud, Aargau, St. Gall, Fribourg, Thurgau, Basle, Soleure, and Schaffhausen. All males above a certain age are electors. The age varies in different cantons from twenty to twenty-five. There are differences also in the age prescribed as necessary to the admission of any one to the senatorial assembly. Property qualification is requisite for members of council in Berne and Aargau. In Soleure, it is only necessary that a candidate should not be a journeyman or servant. In the rest of the cantons last named no qualification is demanded from the legislator any more than the elector. In St. Gall, though there be a representative government, yet all laws are subject to the sanction of the primary assemblies of the communes. Several of the cantons are pure democracies still. The Grisons present a curious example of popular sovereignty. There is a vast number of small districts or parishes, where all the people have a voice in the management of affairs. These are grouped so as to form a certain number of communes. The communes constitute twenty-six hoch gerichts, or higher councils. Above them is the diet of the league; and above all, the diet of the three leagues, which is composed of seventy members, who meet at Coire. The Valais are divided into thirteen dixams or districts, each being a small republic, sending deputies to the cantonal diet, where the Bishop of Sion has four votes. Appenzell is another pure democracy, divided into two separate states, with annual assemblies of all the adult male population. Glarus is equally democratical, but is not divided into districts. Zug is a simple democracy, with a universal assembly every year. Schwyz and Uri are the same. Unterwalden, like Appenzell, consists of two departments, both pure democracies. Neuchâtel is a constitutional monarchy, being part of the dominion of the king of Prussia, who is prince of that canton. The legislative authority is vested in the "*audiences générales*," the members of which are chosen by nearly universal suffrage, except ten deputies who are named by the prince.

Berne, since 1849, has been the permanent place for the meeting of the diet, composed of representatives from the different cantons. The powers of the diet and of the permanent central government now fixed at Berne, where diplomatic business is transacted with foreign ministers, have been already noticed; and it may serve to give some general idea of the state of parties in the diet, if we make the following extract from the work of M. Vieusseux, which, though penned a few years ago, is still correct in its general application. He says: "In the Swiss diet, as well as in other representative assemblies of Europe, the members are divided into three political parties, there known as the right, left, and center. The first-named division consists of the *statu quo* members, or aristocrats, as they are vulgarly called, though in fact this party in Switzerland includes the three forest cantons, the oldest and purest democracies of Switzerland, who are averse to all change in the federal pact, and are jealous and suspicious of the city democracies. The Valais, Neuchâtel, and Basle towns belong also to this division. The left, or radical party, is the party of centralization and unity at the expense of individual independence of the canton; it wishes for a general representative assembly for all Switzerland, elected on the basis of numerical proportion; it is the party of sweeping change, to be effected by numerical majority and physical force. This party was represented in the diet of

1834 by the cantons of Berne, Luzern, Thurgau, Basle country, and St. Gall; not that the population of all these cantons are to be considered as ultra-democratic, but because the ultra-democratic principle prevailed then in their councils, whose function it is to give instructions to the deputies to the diet, which instructions the latter are bound to follow, or ask for further directions. Between the two extreme parties just mentioned is the center, which includes the majority of the cantons; some, however, inclining to the right, others to the left, upon particular questions, but all attached to their cantonal independence, and averse to a general fusion of all Switzerland into a single democracy. The real center, whose device is moderation, conciliation, justice to all, gradual reforms, respect for the cantonal independence, and for existing laws and treaties, was represented in the diet of 1834 by Zurich, Geneva, Vaud, the Grisons, Fribourg, and Glarus." To these statements we may add a remark made in 1851: "Since 1830, democratic principles have made rapid strides in almost all the cantons; and the political constituents of Switzerland at present have, with much truth, been described as consisting of an aristocracy enraged at its own weakness, a democracy eager to ride above them, and demanding for the people more rights than they desire, for doubtful and unknown good, risking all that is most desirable—gentle sway, contented obedience, simplicity of manners, tranquillity of life."

Next to the governments of Switzerland, we would notice the state of education. At Basle and Zurich there are universities; and at Geneva, Berne, and Lausanne, academies, having the power of granting degrees. Two names connected with the University of Basle are familiar to most readers of English theology through translations of their works into our language. The one is De Witte—now no more—a very learned critic, whose opposition to the distinctive truths of the gospel was most decided; the other is Hagenbach, the author of a valuable digest of the history of Christian doctrine. There are several learned societies in Switzerland, in addition to the universities and academies. Such are the Helvetic Society, founded in 1763; the Swiss Society of Public Utility, formed in 1820; and the Natural History Society, established in 1815. The cantonal governments promote popular education; and in this Zurich, Basle, Schaffhausen, Neuchâtel, Geneva, and Vaud, take the lead. The forest cantons are far behind. The same may be said of Appenzell, the Grisons, Ticino, and the Valais. In some of the first-mentioned towns there are normal schools, which exist, too, among the Grisons in Luzern. Most of the head towns of cantons have their gymnasia, in some of which Latin is taught, and other branches of an old-fashioned education; but in the cantons more advanced in the culture of educational methods, modern languages and other departments of a generally useful and accomplished education are introduced. Gymnastic exercises, too, have their proper share of attention in Berne, St. Gall, and Glarus; and in the first of these towns there are mechanical schools for the instruction of artisans. "Switzerland," says Dr. Hoppus, in his "Crisis of Education," "as we learn from the Helvétie, can now boast of having one scholar for every five inhabitants in some parts of the confederation. The cantons of Zurich, Berne, Aargau, Vaud, and St. Gall, are especially named. In Soleure, the ratio in 1837 was stated to be one in nine." "Fribourg has been distinguished by the labors of Père Girard, whose schools in that town were the most successful development of the system of mutual instruction which the continent has yet witnessed. His method resembled, in some important respects, that pursued by Mr. Wood, in the Edinburgh Sessional Schools. Generally it may be stated that the Protestant cantons of Switzerland are nearly foremost in

Europe as respects primary education."—*Recent Measures of Education.* Religious instruction is afforded by the Swiss clergymen. The Protestants have large Sunday schools or catechetical classes, conducted by the ministers, who examine them in the principles of the Helvetic Confession. These juvenile assemblies may be seen gathered in Protestant churches on the noon of the Sabbath, under the superintendence of the pastor, when they are publicly questioned respecting their religious knowledge.

Among the private schools of Switzerland, there is a very remarkable one at Hofwyl near Berne. It was founded by the well-known De Fellenberg, but has undergone some changes, for the worse, we believe, since his death. He was completely devoted to the cause of education, and spent the greater part of his life in promoting it in his native country. Of patrician rank, he counted it no condescension to employ himself in educational efforts, esteeming the formation of youthful character one of the most valuable services which can be rendered to the state as well as to the individual. He divided his establishment into three branches; one for the upper class, a second for the poor, and a third for instruction in practical agriculture. His grand principle was to adapt the education to the natural endowments of the pupil, to endeavor to fit him for that thing which it would appear God meant him for; and the peculiar method which he adopted, and which tended much to the successful working of the schools while he lived, was to nourish and encourage a public spirit in the establishment on the side of obedience and all virtue—a spirit which he had carefully nursed at the outset of his enterprise, by beginning with a very few whom he imbued with his own sentiments. As fresh pupils were added, they were brought under the existing influence and molded accordingly, and any boy found to remain decidedly out of sympathy with his companions was expelled. De Fellenberg employed a large number of assistants, and sometimes, in cases of peculiar idiosyncrasy, would appoint one tutor to the oversight of a single child. He treated his pupils as a father, and ever appealed to their love rather than their fears. Many of the details of his plans would be impracticable with us, and some things about his establishment would be found objectionable; but we cannot help thinking that the principles and spirit of that great educational undertaking which has rendered him illustrious in his own country, deserve far more attention than they have yet received in this.

Before we proceed to another topic connected

with society in Switzerland, we would refer to a very singular fact mentioned in the introduction to Murray's Swiss Hand-book, which will serve as a connecting link between the present and the following subject: "A singular custom, connected with education, prevails in some parts of Switzerland, which deserves notice here from the influence which it exercises over society. In many of the large towns, children of the same age and sex are associated together by their parents in little knots and clubs called *Sociétés de Dimanche.* The parents seek out for their children an eligible set of companions when they are still quite young. The parties so formed amount to twelve or fifteen in number, and the variation of age between them is not more than two or three years. All the members meet in turn on Sunday evenings at the houses of their parents, while children, to play together and partake of tea-cakes and sweetmeats, attended by their bonnes, or nurses; when grown up, to pass the evening in other occupations and amusements suited to their age. At these meetings, not even brothers or sisters are present, except they are members of the society. From thus being constantly thrown together on all occasions, a strict friendship grows up among the members of each brotherhood or sisterhood, which generally lasts through life, even after the people are settled and dispersed about the world. The females, even when grown up, distinguish their companions by such endearing terms as, 'Ma mignonne,' 'Mon cœur,' 'Mon ange.' This practice renders Swiss society very exclusive, and few strangers, however well introduced, penetrate below the surface."

The last remark in the foregoing extract will prepare the reader for not expecting any account of the private social life of the Swiss. We do not pretend to give any information on that subject; our own observations have been made only in public, and we should regard inferences relative to domestic habits and the privacies of home life very untrustworthy, if derived only from what a traveler may see of a people in places of general resort. We may just remark that the western Swiss, in their social character and habits, assimilate to the French; the eastern and northern to the Germans of the Tyrol and Suabia. The French language is spoken in the former, the German or dialects of German in the latter. We believe that there is a strong line of caste in some of the large Swiss towns, but have been informed by residents that among people of the same class there is a great deal of neighborly feeling and cheerful fellowship.

Our own notices of social life in Switzerland

have been confined to the hotel, the pension or boarding-house, and the bathing establishments. In the hotel one meets with persons from all parts of the world, and almost everything distinctively Swiss is there merged. The *table d'hôte* is generally a scene of much interest to a stranger, affording, as it often does, a gathering of many nations—the English and Americans being in some cases predominant. Such a place as the hotel on the top of the Righi, where a hundred people or so assemble in the evening, to prepare for witnessing the morrow's sunrise, is preëminently favorable to the exhibition of social habits pertaining to the respective travelers; for there, especially, reserve is thrown off, and the costumes, and manners, and conversation in many languages, producing a very discordant hubbub, are extremely amusing. In the best hotels there is no want of comforts and luxuries. The *pension*, where persons are accommodated with everything at so many francs a day, and meet in a common room for meals and occasional intercourse, is less public than the hotel, and makes a nearer approach to family life. In some of these the English are most numerous; in some the Germans; in some the French: and they bring with them the habits of their own country. The fare is according to the pay, and of course the social pleasure derived, according to the company. We have pleasant reminiscences of a pension at Interlachen, where the arrangements were quite Swiss, and the visitors mostly German, the tables well spread, the party agreeable—the waiters being daughters of the hostess, in the costume of the canton. The Swiss bathing establishments are great gathering places for people seeking health, or striving to preserve it. We have visited two, very different in character; the one is the bath of Pfeffers, most romantic in position, and crushed in between lofty rocks, where they nearly close up the valley of the Tamina. The mountain gorge, in which the bath is situated, is truly frightful, and the buildings are very gloomy. The springs are hot, and pour out clouds of steam. There are long passages and wide halls, and dining-rooms and dormitories, and bathing-cells in abundance, giving the place very much the aspect of a conventual establishment, with invalids, very melancholy in appearance, slowly and quietly moving up and down like monks. The house, from its position, must at all times be very gloomy; but what rays of cheerfulness may be thrown over it by good society we cannot say, as our visit was very brief, and we went to see the springs and the scenery, not the people. We may remark in passing, that we have seen nothing in Switzerland surpassing the baths of Pfeffers for stern and savage grandeur compressed into a point. The valley or gorge beyond the baths, leading to the springs by a little rickety modern bridge beside the foaming torrent, with the rocks lapping one another overhead—all so gloomy, and the roaring of the waters so tremendous—is certainly one which no traveler in that part of Switzerland should omit to enter. The baths of Leuk, at the foot of the Gemmi Pass, are very different. When we were there, all looked as cheerful as in the other case all was melancholy. The former was Il Penseroso, and the latter L'Allegro. There are eighteen or twenty bathing-houses at Leuk.

The Swiss are fond of festive gatherings, some of which on certain occasions are of national interest, and afford striking displays of characteristic costumes, manners, and habits. In most of the cantons there are societies for archery and rifle-shooting, the marksman's skill being of much practical importance to the children of the mountain, who are wont to bring down the chamois as it climbs the perilous heights. Wrestling, too, and other athletic exercises are much practiced in some parts, and have also societies formed to patronize and promote them. Exhibitions of skill and power in all these respects take place annually in the chief towns of the district where the societies are established; and then there are prizes—some very considerable—distributed to those who excel in these rustic feats. But of all the Swiss festivities, "*La Fête des Vignerons*" at Vevay is the most celebrated. The vineyards of the vicinity are very rich, and yield some of the choicest wines of Switzerland. The cultivation of the grape here is as ancient as Roman times, and a temple to Bacchus is known to have stood near Vevay, from the discovery of a stone there bearing the inscription, "*Libero Patri Colliensi.*" A society has existed from remote times for promoting the best husbandry of the vine, and at spring and autumn persons are sent out, well skilled and of experience, to examine the produce of the district. Medals and pruning hooks are given as prizes to the most successful cultivators. At distant intervals grand feasts are held under the direction of this ancient guild, and these are "*Les Fêtes des Vignerons.*" One took place in 1797; another in 1819; in 1833, again there was a festival; the last was in 1851. Murray, in his Guide-Book, gives an account of the manner in which the ceremonies, processions, and festivities used to be performed, and they seem to have included an odd and irreverent mixture of classical and sacred associations—father Bacchus and Silenus being accompanied by Noah and his ark. At the last celebration, from an account given in the "Illustrated News," and from the report of a friend who was present, we learn that the old customs were somewhat modified; the personages appearing in the procession being all classical or rustic representatives of the four seasons; and these with archers and vine-dressers, and many shows, formed the procession. In the market-place of Vevay, there were public ceremonies in the midst of a vast amphitheater, crowded with spectators, including the coronation of the most successful vine-dressers, the singing of odes, and dancing. These festive scenes were extended through two days, and the whole was closed by a public illumination. Forty thousand persons are reported to have been present at the last fête, and from all accounts it must have been a remarkable manifestation of national character. The motto of the guild is "*Ora et labora*," pray and labor—an excellent maxim. How far the first piece of wisdom may be practically regarded by the Swiss vine-dressers we cannot say; their attention to the second is very obvious; and, assuredly, a diligent attention to both will be found the true path to prosperity: as in vine-dressing, so in everything else.

In turning to look for a moment to other and more important forms of society, to those which are exhibited in the churches of the country, we may remark that the Roman Catholics of Switzerland form about two-fifths of the population; being, according to the census of 1850, nine hundred and seventy-one thousand eight hundred and twenty.* The three old forest cantons, together with Luzern, Zug, the Valais, and Ticino, are thoroughly Roman Catholic, and did not (un-

* A valuable table of religious statistics as to Switzerland is given in a volume just published, called "The Religious Condition of Christendom," containing papers read before the Evangelical Alliance in London, 1851. That table has subjoined the following summary remark:—"In every thousand persons five hundred and ninety-three would be Reformed, four hundred and six Catholics, and one Jew,—three Reformed to two Catholics. The proportion borne by the Reformed to the Roman Catholic population remains much as it was, notwithstanding the accession of the Valais, Neuchâtel, and Geneva in 1815, and the various degrees in which the population of the different cantons has increased. The Roman Catholic population has decreased and the Reformed increased in the cantons of Berne, Glarus, St. Gall, and Argovie; while, on the contrary, the Reformed has decreased and the Roman Catholics increased in the Grisons, Thurgovie, the city and canton of Basle, Neuchâtel, and Geneva, especially in the latter canton." As to language—the German is spoken by 1,670,000; the French by 474,000; the Italian by 133,500; and the Romauch by 45,000.

til very lately) tolerate any other religion than their own, except that in Luzern the opening of a Protestant chapel was permitted; but matters are now altered, and religious liberty, to some extent, is enjoyed in all the cantons.* In St. Gall the Roman Catholics are a majority; and the same is the case in Fribourg and Soleure; but in all these cantons Protestants are allowed the right of worship, and in St. Gall they enjoy per-

* The federal constitution of 1848 grants the free exercise of worship, but only to *recognized* Christian confessions; so that Dissenters might be prohibited throughout the whole extent of the confederation from the exercise of worship under the pretense of maintaining public order. "Besides, although the same constitution guarantees to all Swiss belonging to a Christian Church the right of settling in any part of the Swiss territory, a permit of abode has just been withdrawn from an evangelical schoolmaster residing at Martigny in Valais, who has hitherto appealed in vain to the federal authority. The present state of things, therefore, leaves much to be desired in respect to religious liberty, though we acknowledge with satisfaction that the cause is making progress dayly. A visible change has taken place in the minds of many, especially in the Canton de Vaud, the only quarter in which a retrograde movement in this matter has been made. The Free Church can now assemble anywhere without molestation, for which we thank God."—*Condition of Christendom*, p. 559.

fect civil equality. In the other cantons Roman Catholics are in a minority; in some a very small one; but in all they have freely conceded to them the same liberties as other subjects. In the Roman Catholic districts the parishes generally are smaller than in the Protestant; and owing to this circumstance, and to that of several priests being attached to one establishment, the number of the Roman Catholic clergy far exceeds that of the Protestant, though the flocks of the latter comprise three-fifths of the population. In Roman Catholic Switzerland there is a priest for about every hundred and fifty persons. In the Protestant portions of the country there is one to every seven hundred. There are five thousand two hundred priests and monks, and two thousand nuns.* The convents are sixty in number; among which are St. Urban in Luzern, Weltingen in Aargau, and Einsiedeln in the canton of Schwyz. The last is a place of high repute among papists, on account of a black image of the Virgin which it contains, miraculous and celestial in its origin, as some believe. Immense multitudes flock to this famous shrine, and it has been calculated that between the years 1820 and 1840, the average annual resort of pilgrims has been one hun-

* These numbers are taken from statistics published within the last twenty years.

dred and fifty thousand. The spot still retains its popularity, and swarms of devotees may be often seen wending their way to its altars. The most absurd superstitions are there cherished; and it is actually pretended that from one of the jets of the fountain in front of the church, our Saviour drank when he was upon earth. How this could be is not explained, and by the ignorant devotees is not inquired. In Aargau, where the population is mixed and the Protestants are most numerous, efforts have been made to reform conventual abuses, but the opposition has been very obstinate. "In the mountain districts," observes Dr. Alexander, "Catholicism appears in much the same guise as it bore before the Reformation; it is the religion of an honest, untutored, and superstitious race, who receive it in all its integrity, submit to it with undisguised sincerity,* and regard with horror all who would

* Both the influence of the priests and the superstition of the people were remarkably manifested during the late wars of the Sunderbund. The former blessed the bullets and fire-arms, the latter believed that in the sacerdotal benediction they received a charm that would secure them from danger. The continued sympathy with the Sunderbund movement, at least in the neighborhood to which it relates, appears from the following anecdote, recorded in the "Religious Condition of Christendom:—" A fête lately

call it in question. In the Italian States there is more of astuteness, more of mere formalism, less depth of feeling and sincerity of devotion, but not less of bigotry or ignorance. In the French cantons Catholicism appears under a more cosmopolitan guise; it is the religion of a people acquainted with letters, accustomed to the usages of cultivated society, apt to be assailed by argument directed against their faith, and consequently more versed in crafty devices and plausible reasonings. The Jesuits, who ever since the foundation of their order have been the main stay of the Church of Rome, though their atrocious proceedings at times have excited the indignation of Roman Catholic sovereigns, and brought down the condemnation of the pontiff himself, have long been an active party in Switzerland, seeking to propagate as well as secure the Roman Catholic faith, and for that end engaging in deep

brought together the whole population of a district in Fribourg, in the confines of the Canton de Vaud. Suddenly a man steps forward, with proud and confident looks, and, with a glass in his hand, announces that he is going to propose a toast, which, without exception, will make all hearts beat:—'To the Seven Cantons of the Sunderbund,' said he; and the multitude, lately divided into two parties, Radical and Romish, answered to his voice by an immense and unanimous applause."

political intrigues, and in some instances plunging the country into civil war. Their head-quarters are at Fribourg; and in Soleure, Schwyz, and the Valais they are strong and active. In the last of these cantons they procured, so late as the year 1845, the passing of a law proscribing all assemblies, discussions, and conversations reflecting on the Roman Catholic Church, under penalty of fine and imprisonment. The law also prohibited the possession of any book *indirectly* attacking the religion of the state; so that, for having any book whatever which the Jesuit priest might pronounce unfriendly to Roman Catholicism, a person might be amenable to the authorities. A Swiss writer has justly said, "The Jesuits are the enemies of Switzerland, because they hate and would obliterate Swiss feeling and Swiss nationality. They are the enemies of Switzerland, because they detest and aim at overthrowing its freedom. They are the enemies of Switzerland, because wherever they are, they try to appropriate the civil power, to abrogate institutions, and to degrade the Swiss people into the condition of slaves under a priestocracy. In fine, they are the enemies of Switzerland, because they oppose all true intellectual education, and would put chains on men's minds, that they may the more easily enslave their persons."

In the Roman Catholic cantons, there is less general intelligence and a much lower order of civilization than in those that are Protestant. The fact cannot be denied by any one who has mixed with the Swiss, or who has traveled through the country, and noticed the most obvious indications of the state of the people. Passing from the canton of Berne to the canton of the Valais, the tourist finds himself in a different region, as it regards the state of the farms, the gardens, the villages, the towns, the houses, and the people; neatness, and cleanliness, and order, and evident physical comfort and prosperity, are at once changed for their opposites. Roman Catholics themselves have been forced to admit the fact, and an intelligent writer among them, Franscini, in his Statutes of the Swiss, attributes it to the number of ecclesiastics, who are so many citizens withdrawn from secular employments—to the absorption of property by monasteries—to the large sums spent in worship—and to the numerous saints' days observed as holidays by the people. These things, no doubt, in some degree, lead to and promote the evil in question, and are themselves evils, whatever Roman Catholics may think of them; nor does the writer just mentioned attempt to deny the neglect of education in the Roman Catholic cantons—another fact damaging the Church to which they belong. But over and above all this, is there not a spirit in Popery which serves to crush the energies of a people, and to retard their progress to the highest state of civilization? Witness *every* country where Popery has all things its own way—witness the papal states, which of course must be the model for Roman Catholic Christendom. Three-fifths of the Swiss are nominally Protestant; and according to the last census, in 1850, amounted to one million four hundred and seventeen thousand four hundred and seventy-four. The cantons of Zurich, Basle, Berne, Vaud, Neuchâtel, and Geneva, are those in which Protestantism is most prevalent. In Aargau, Appenzell, Glarus, Schaffausen, and Thurgau, there is also a majority of Protestants; yet in all, the principle of equality in civil rights is maintained in reference to the Roman Catholic part of the population. The Protestant clergy may amount to seventeen hundred, and very few parishes have more than one minister. "There is no Swiss national Church; but in each canton, that formula of doctrine and order which has seemed best to the ruling powers has been established by public sanction. In respect of doctrine there is no great difference, so far as creeds go, between the different cantonal Churches, almost all of them holding professedly by the ancient Helvetic confession; and in point of order they are more or less strictly conformed to the Presbyterian model, though in some cases with a slight infusion of the Episcopal element, and in others with certain leanings to the Congregational system. Thus, as respects the appointment of the ministers, in some cantons the choice rests exclusively with the people, who have power to appoint and power to remove, independent of any superior control; in other cantons the government nominates the clergy, and the people have not a veto on the appointment; in other cases, the people send up a list to the government, with whom the final appointment rests; in some cases a right of interference belongs to the body of clergy already in office; and in one case, that of Neuchâtel, the clerical body absorb the entire power, subject only to the supervision of the king of Prussia, who never interferes with their movements. For the most part, the Presbyterian parity is preserved among the clergy, the office of *doyen*, which is the highest rank among them, being simply that of *primus inter pares*, the first among equals, and lasting but for one year at a time in the case of each occupant. In the canton of Basle, however, some vestiges of the episcopal subordination are retained; the first minister of the Minster Church, in the city of Basle, holding a certain official preëminence among his brethren; and his colleague, the second minister, bearing the title of archidiaconus, or archdeacon. The tenure by which the ministers hold their parishes is also very different in different cantons, some being elected for life, or until any fault worthy of deposition is committed; others for a term of years; and others from week to week. In fine, the mode in which the clergy are supported varies in different cantons; in some the government provides the entire salary of the minister, while in others the government supplies only a part, and in some cases but a very small part, and the rest is made up by fees, or from the voluntary offerings of the people.*

The state of religion in the Protestant Churches of Switzerland, as compared with that among the Roman Catholics, is by no means such as to produce much complacency. A state of mind

* This general view is supplied by Dr. Alexander, but the Churches of Switzerland are in such a transition state, that what may apply to them one year may be incorrect another. For example, Professor Baup tells the Evangelical Alliance in 1851: "The Bernese Church has *just received* a mixed synodical organization, of which it is to make trial some time before it is definitely adopted. You see," he adds, "we occupy a shifting position—the picture we draw to-day may possibly be considerably changed to-morrow."

scarcely better than infidelity or skepticism obtains extensively among those who bear the name of the Reformed. Sincerity and earnestness under any religious form is but rare with the Swiss Protestants; this is the opinion of those who have had the best opportunities of inquiry and observation. "Dead forms," says Dr. Alexander, to whose work on the religious state of Switzerland we are in this part of our volume greatly indebted, —"Dead forms, parchment orthodoxy, mechanical rites, engross the entire religious interest of multitudes; and with others a lax indifferentism and courteous latitudinarianism confound all religious distinctions, and make religion itself a mere article of worldly convenience.* Between these two

* In a paper on Infidelity in Switzerland, read at the Evangelical Alliance meeting in 1851, it was stated that in French Switzerland, that is, Geneva, the High Jura, Vaud, Neuchâtel, and Berne, where all have their children baptized, who are afterward admitted to the Lord's supper, many never enter the church after their first communion. "Even among those who remain more faithful for a time," proceeds the writer, the Rev. L. Burnier, "open infidelity soon reaps a new harvest; so that a great majority of our artisans and manufacturers end in throwing off all regard to divine worship. Their infidelity is open, avowed, reasoned, or rather nibbling at arguments, (I speak in a general manner;) hence it follows that it is more varied than among the country people. At one time it is the con-

classes the great mass of those who still adhere to the profession of Protestant Christianity in the national Churches of Switzerland are divided. The exceptions are comparatively few, and are found principally among the younger clergy. The brightness of some of these exceptions is such as almost to compensate for the gloom amid which they shine." These statements are confirmed by other authorities—by the Rev. R. Burgess, for example, who was once a resident in Geneva, and who, after speaking favorably of the canton of Vaud, adds, "There is much sound religion in the cantons of Basle and Berne. The state of the Reformed religion, viewed in the mass of professing Protestants, is gloomy; viewed in its reviving energy, and among the handful of pious believers, whose zeal is worthy of the primitive ages, it is cheering and consoling." The re-

fession of faith of the Savoyard vicar, at another it is the cynical mocking of Voltairianism; but among people who are upward of forty years of age, infidelity is the fierce and full representation of the irreligious and revolutionary movement of the eighteenth century—an infidelity entirely French, that of Volney, whose works are often found in our workshops; but among those of a new generation, it is the pantheistic mysticism of Lamennais, or of Pierre Leroux, and the socialist materialism, which its skillful advocates cover over with a kind of Gallo-Germanism."

sult of our own inquiries when in Switzerland was to the same effect. To speak with indignity of Christ crucified, and to exhibit him merely as a good and great man, was lately no very uncommon thing with the Swiss teachers of theology in public; and it may be stated that, some years ago, the professor of divinity at Geneva published an essay *against* original sin—the Trinitarian system—and justification by faith, and that, too, without a word of remonstrance from his University or ecclesiastical brethren. The latter excused their silence by saying, that every man in their Church had a right to entertain and publish his own opinions. The men, on the other hand, who, in the established Churches of Switzerland are doing their divine Master's work by the simple and earnest preaching of his word, and the ingathering of souls into his fold, are less known to European fame; but their witness is above—their record is on high. The doctrinal errors, the semi-infidelity, the absence of discipline and the want of life in the old religious communities of Switzerland, some time ago awakened deep concern in the minds of those with whom Christianity had become more than a form. In Geneva especially was this the case. The visits of pious foreigners to that city, particularly Mr. Robert Haldane and Mr. Henry Drummond, promoted the revival of vital piety, which before their arrival had commenced, and they encouraged those whose spirits had been touched by a holy zeal to stem the progress of falsehood and corruption. In 1816, an Anglican congregation was formed in Geneva by the present bishop of Winchester, "and it became," says Mr. Burgess, "a city of refuge for many who were deprived of the means of grace in their own community." In 1817, a formal secession took place from the Genevese establishment, and a new religious community was formed under M. Bost, M. Empeytaz, and Mr. Guers. In 1819, through the preaching of the well-known Cæsar Malan, another secession took place, but he still remained in the old Genevan Church. At length he was expelled for his doctrinal teaching, and then, in 1823, he formed a distinct Church on the Presbyterian plan, and erected a chapel at Pré l'Evêque, one of the suburbs of Geneva. In the mean time, another congregation was formed; for, in 1819, M. Gaussen and M. Cellerier, by a publication on the Helvetic Confession, roused the displeasure of the venerable company of pastors, as the ecclesiastical government was called—a circumstance which ended in the suspension of the former from his clerical functions. At the same time, M. Merle d'Aubigné and M. Galland arrived in Geneva, who, sympathizing with M. Gaussen, united with him in the formation of the Société Evangélique de Genève, the most influential religious body now in that city. Their place of worship is the Oratoire, where the congregation is large, and the gospel preached with earnestness and simplicity; and connected with it is a theological school, of which M. Merle d'Aubigné and M. Gaussen are professors.

The religious awakening at Geneva soon spread over other cantons, and in 1824 evangelical Churches were formed in the canton de Vaud, and places extending to Neuchâtel. Laxity of discipline in the national establishment was among the chief causes of their secession, and the ecclesiastical organizations which have sprung out of the proceeding have been remarkable for the strictness of their rules respecting admission to the Lord's table. The purity of their doctrine and the earnestness of their piety have been equally conspicuous; and in some of the early stages of their history, when they had to suffer much for conscience' sake, there were afforded among them beautiful examples of Christian constancy and heroism. Not only had they to suffer from unjust laws and tribunals, but popular fury was let loose against them, and their houses were attacked and their persons assailed with cruel violence. M. Tuvet was banished, and from exposure to cold, insult, and privation, from imprisonment and ruthless attacks by savage mobs, he became so enfeebled and diseased that life was cut short, and in the prospect of his departure he prayed for his persecutors, and said to Dr. Malan, who asked him whether he was happy in the prospect of death, "How can I do otherwise than rejoice in the expectation of so soon beholding Him who has so loved me?" In 1847, a free evangelical Church was established in the canton de Vaud, adopting an organization which seems to blend together both Presbyterian and Congregational elements. About forty societies have adopted this constitution, and the whole number of members reported in October, 1850, was three thousand one hundred.

Other religious communities in Switzerland have of late years appeared, of varied character, including not only Independents, Baptists, and Wesleyans, but congregations of the Plymouth brethren, followers of the late Mr. Irving, and persons holding what is called Lardonism, from a minister of the name of Lardon, who, in endeavoring to adhere to apostolic usage, adopted some curious peculiarities, such as refusing to shave, and always sending letters by hand instead of through the post.

In the national Churches, of late, there has been an improvement. The clergy of the canton de Vaud are now generally orthodox. The same may be said of the ministers of Neuchâtel, where, though more life is wanted in the pulpit, yet it is pleasing to notice that extra meetings are held for religious edification during the week, attended in some cases by large congregations. The weekly meeting in the town of Neuchâtel sometimes numbers as many as five hundred persons. In several villages there are meetings, where missions and other evangelical methods of usefulness are brought before the people.* Geneva, too, has made some advance in the right direction. The company of pastors have dropped their old opposition to evangelical truth, and have become active in promoting the better observance of the Sabbath, in establishing deaconries to aid pastoral work, and in instituting an evening service. The last accounts we have seen from Geneva, and which are so late as February 17, 1853, confirm what we have stated on the authority of Professor Baup, and even furnish additional

* These notices are taken from the work before quoted, published by the Alliance. The paper relates only to French Switzerland. It gives by no means an encouraging account of Berne, but mentions a zealous and active pastor laboring in Fribourg

grounds of hope. A memoir has recently been published by a student of the national academy of Geneva, which presents a glowing report of the present condition of the Genevese Church. But a writer in the "Christian Times," (March 4, 1853,) more moderately observes, in reference to the subject:—

"I joyfully acknowledge that the Genevese population are characterized by greater seriousness; that the present, and still less the past state of things satisfies nobody; that the necessity is felt of having positive doctrines; that greater freedom is allowed in the choice of subjects for the pulpit; that the consistory and the company of pastors make laudable efforts to remedy the existing evil—to awaken life in their flocks; that this latter body has divided itself into several committees, which propose to 'develop the knowledge of the religious life by various means;' that they have established Sunday evening services; that they have 'regulated religious instruction;' that they have laid down the rule 'that the pastors shall henceforth undertake the instruction of their catechumens;' that 'religious literature' has been enriched with several works, which give indications of improvement," etc. And he further adds what, coming from a person on the spot, and one who evidently possesses a discriminating mind and a Christian judgment, is very encouraging :—

"I am, then, gratified to be able to agree with the author of the Memoir,—

"1. That the number of serious Christians in the national Church is dayly increasing, and that they will at length make themselves heard, unless they should be pressed into the ranks of dissent, as was imprudently done in former cases.

"2. That the clergy are endeavoring to awaken and maintain a certain Christian activity, which will grow in depth and in beneficial results, in proportion as they occupy themselves less with their own interests as a body, and more exclusively with those which relate to the Church of Christ at large.

"3. That we must acknowledge all the good they are instrumental in accomplishing, and regard it as the dawn of better days, praying with all fervor that He who has commenced the good work will finish it, for this he alone can do.

"4. While cherishing the most sincere desire for the realization of the hopes of our young friend, the author of the Memoir, with respect to this Church in travail, and which we all love, in every direction prayer is ascending to Him who holds the hearts of men in his hand, and turns them as rivers of water, that the real Christians who, in less auspicious days, took refuge in free and dissenting Churches, may have their hearts increasingly enlarged toward their brethren from whom they are for a while separated; that they may be drawn toward them by their common affections and sympathies, and by the loving evangelical spirit of the Master to whom they belong; that they may forget the past, with its unhappy associations; and that they may, without hesitation, hold out the right hand of fellowship to those whom they see embracing their convictions that there remains something to be achieved in this respect; and that it should be remembered that if, with some of their own number, the truth which saves was revealed in a moment; many—and indeed most—have had their eyes opened to the light by degrees, and the truth has only reached them 'line upon line, and precept upon precept.'"

With this imperfect notice of the religious condition of some parts of Switzerland we must close this volume. Art and society, certain developments of which we have described in this second part of our work, afford illustrations of the presence and power in our world of the everlasting God, and should inspire devout reflections in the mind of the reader and the traveler. We look through the intermediate agencies, voluntary though they be, which have fashioned the forms of art, and have worked out the results of society, to the recognition of Him who has given to man the wisdom and the will to produce so much that is fair, wonderful, and grand. We must confess that in traveling, as we look on fine buildings, and ramble through the streets of busy cities, and investigate ingenious contrivances, and inquire into modes of government, and listen to various kinds of human speech, we are deeply impressed with the idea of a divine cause as the basis of the busy working of human causes. The element of conscious and free action only heightens our adoring wonder at the ways of Him who can make, and preserve, and multiply a world full of agents, such as human beings are. The crowds working with thought and will, are still in the very act of executing their own designs, subservient to the accomplishment of the purpose of Him who created them, and are among the wonderful manifestations of his power and glory. Subject as men are to the government of the Most High, as having conscience, as being amenable to laws, and as standing with the prospect of another world before them, how clearly does religion appear to be absolutely needful to give completeness to their character, safety to their condition, and happiness to their future existence! As fallen and degenerate beings, which observation and Scripture prove them to be, what but the remedies provided in the gospel can replace them in the right relation to the Lord of the universe, and restore in their hearts the fealty and love they owe to him? These remedies are all-sufficient. Man's nature is corrupt; but the gospel reveals a scheme for its renewal, through the regenerating influences of the Holy Spirit, freely imparted to all who aright seek them. Is he exposed to the condemnation of a violated law, which demands a perfect obedience? The gospel points to One who has fulfilled that law, and who, having wrought out a perfect righteousness, now calls on men everywhere to repent, and to receive the remission of sins through faith in his blood? Are man's affections depraved and selfish? The gospel proclaims a mode in which they may be restored to their proper objects. Justified by faith, the soul has peace with God and joy in the Holy Ghost, and walking in the path of holiness, is renewed in the image of its Lord and Saviour. Thus, delivered out of the state of confusion, contradiction, and falsehood, which results from sin, the mind will take "fresh interest in art and society, because these things will then be seen in new and higher relations, and connected with vaster and nobler issues."

But we cannot complete our volume on Switzerland without falling back upon thoughts of its glorious scenery, which makes so much more powerful an impression upon the traveler than either its forms of art or its modifications of society. Perhaps no country in the world is so *crowded* with objects beautiful and sublime. It is not only here and there, but almost everywhere, that one meets with something to arrest attention and inspire delight; and the remembrance of the whole, till the parts are arranged and grouped into order by a careful patient memory, is full of bewildering magnificence and glory.

The things that artists strive to paint and poets love to praise—the emerald-paved valleys, and the wild-flowing streams, and the fir-mantled hills, and the diamond-dusted snows, and the azure-tinted glaciers, and cloud-wrapped lofty solitudes—all these, and many more, come sweeping before the imagination in glowing vision, as one sits and muses over by-gone rambles in that land of beauty, power, and wonder.

And then over all is seen the shadow of that Hand which molded the mountain, and scooped out the channel of the river, and planted the forest, and dappled with rich colors the field and the meadow, the rock and the cloud.

And, moreover, images are left in the mind "which exist not by themselves, but are sanctified by many a holy association."

The idea is well and forcibly expressed in the following passage taken from a work entitled "Scenes in Other Lands, with their Associations," by John Stoughton:—

"They embody the ethereal; they give color to the spiritual; they form the setting of precious thoughts, which come not from nature, but from the word of the Lord of nature. Ours is a marvelous world in this respect as well as others—that it is so framed as to become suggestive, illustrative, and monumental of the facts, and laws, and principles of the spiritual universe. What of divine truth is there that has been ever discerned by the reason of man, either as revealed in the constitution of nature or on the pages of the Bible, but it has found its symbol, type, and picture in material things? The whole material creation, if we may repeat what we have indicated before, is a sublime allegory. Earth, and seas, and skies are covered with hieroglyphics. The prophecies and songs of the Bible, the parables of our Lord Jesus Christ, point to this. Many a valley and hill, many a rock, and how many a flower and bud, once seen, remain to us forever after a sign and note of a thought higher than itself, like the remembered vision of the Cloud Bridge, which a poet has thus described:"—

> "Saw ye that cloud which arose in the west,
> As the burning sun sank down to his rest—
> How it spread so wide, and tower'd so high
> O'er the molten gold of that glowing sky,
> That it seem'd—O! it seem'd like some archèd way,
> As it beam'd and gleam'd in that glorious ray,
> Where the spirit, freed
> From its earthly weed,
> And robed in the white
> Of the saints in light,
> Might pass from the waves of sin and woe,
> To that world where ceaseless pleasures flow?
>
> "Ye saw that cloud—how it tower'd alone,
> Like an archèd path o'er the billows thrown;
> How its pillars of azure and purple stood,
> And mock'd at the dash of the angry flood,
> While it beam'd—O! it beam'd from its battlements high,
> As it gleam'd and stream'd in that western sky
> Such a flood of mellow and golden light
> As chain'd and fix'd the ravish'd sight,
> And pour'd along our dark'ning way
> The peace and joy of celestial day.
>
> "Such, as we haste to our heavenly home,
> Saviour! such be the sights that come,—
> Thus, while the visions of time flit by,
> And the fashion of earth grows dim to our eye,

Thus let the light—O! the light of thy love,
Beam bright on our sight from the mansions above—
    Rending the gloom
    Which inwraps the tomb,
    And guiding our eye
    To that world on high
Where the people who love Thee forever shall share
The rest thou hast purchased, and gone to prepare."

THE END.

Stories from the History of England.

Stories from the History of England. 2 vols.

18mo., pp. 216, 278. Price, each........... $0 30

Irish Stories.

Irish Stories, for Thoughtful Readers.

18mo., pp. 285. Price....................... $0 30

Three Days on the Ohio.

Three Days on the Ohio River. By Father William.

18mo., pp. 60. Price........................ $0 16

Two Fortunes.

The Two Fortunes: or, Profession and Practice.

18mo., pp. 116. Price....................... $0 20

The Tempest.

The Tempest: or, an Account of the Nature, Properties, Dangers, and Uses of Wind in various parts of the World.

18mo., pp. 231. Price....................... $0 27

Kenneth Forbes.

Kenneth Forbes: or, Fourteen Ways of Studying the Bible.

18mo., pp. 298. Price....................... $0 30

Rambles in the South.

Rambles in the South. By Father William.

18mo., pp. 196. Price....................... $0 25

Sketches of Mission Life in Oregon.

Sketches of Mission Life in Oregon.

18mo., pp. 229. Price....................... $0 27

Frank Harrison.

The History of a Wayward Boy.

18mo., pp. 150. Price..................... $0 20

Old Edinburgh.

A Historical Sketch of th. Ancient Metropolis of Scotland.

18mo., pp. 208. Price..................... $0 24

Australia:

Its Scenery, Natural History, and Resources. With a Glance at its Gold Fields.

18mo., pp. 207. Price..................... $0 24

The Withered Leaf;

Or, Recollections of a Little Girl.

18mo., pp. 176. Price..................... $0 22

Greek and Eastern Churches:

Their History, Faith, and Worship.

18mo., pp. 220. Price..................... $0 24

Youth's Monitor, Vol. 2.

18mo., pp. 288. Price..................... $0 28

The Checkered Scene;

Or, Memorials of Samuel Oliver. By Rev. GERVASE SMITH.

18mo., p[illegible] Price..................... $0 21

Youth's Monitor, Vol. 3.

18mo., pp. 288. Price..................... $0 28

Youth's Monitor, Vol. 4.

18mo., pp. 288. Price..................... $0 28

www.ingramcontent.com/pod-product-compliance
Lightning Source LLC
LaVergne TN
LVHW011204110826
845150LV00006B/1320

* 9 7 8 1 4 2 5 5 1 8 5 3 0 *